White Noise

An A–Z of the Contradictions in Cyberculture

Andrew Calcutt

First published 1999 by
MACMILLAN PRESS LTD
Houndmills, Basingstoke, Hampshire RG21 6XS
and London
Companies and representatives
throughout the world

ISBN 0–333–69955–6 hardcover
ISBN 0–333–69956–4 paperback

A catalogue record for this book is available
from the British Library.

This book is printed on paper suitable for recycling and
made from fully managed and sustained forest sources.

10   9   8   7   6   5   4   3   2   1
08   07   06   05   04   03   02   01   00   99

Printed and bound in Great Britain by
Antony Rowe Ltd, Chippenham, Wiltshire

Published in the United States of America by
ST. MARTIN'S PRESS, INC.,
Scholarly and Reference Division
175 Fifth Avenue, New York, N.Y. 10010

ISBN 0–312–21660–2 clothbound
ISBN 0–312–21661–0 paperback

For Alka, Cora and our future

Contents

Preface

As a commentator on cyberculture for various magazines, and as a commissioning editor at Channel Cyberia, I have ploughed through many written accounts of the Internet which have attempted to reach a singular conclusion about its impact on society. Some accounts have claimed that the advent of the Internet is a boon to humanity which can free us from the constraints of the material world. Others have argued that the Internet is itself a form of constraint, either because it provides the powerful with a new means of coercing the powerless, or because it acts as a 'narcotic' fantasy-world which diverts people from reality.

It seems to me that neither of these accounts is sufficient. Each version involves a highly selective form of reporting, which leaves out the facts that do not fit the thesis. Moreover, both versions invest digital communications, and the Internet in particular, with an autonomous momentum that they simply do not have.

Most of the published histories of cyberculture begin with the technology and then move on to examine its application in society. Thus current trends in society are usually described as if they are effects which have been caused by the new technology. Hence we are said to be living in 'the Information Age'. But technology can only be developed and applied in accordance with the social context from which it is derived. Technology which does not correspond to the mood of the times is likely to be discarded, or never developed in the first place, regardless of how beneficial it might be. Moreover, it frequently happens that the same technical devices are applied and re-applied in various ways in different historical contexts, to the point where subsequent applications bear little or no resemblance to the original usage.

For example, the electric guitar in fifties rock'n'roll sounds nothing like the original electrified guitars as played in the thirties; nor did the latter connote the rebel–outlaw sensibility which probably reached its peak in the late sixties during the career of 'guitar-hero' Jimi Hendrix. Similarly, the Internet of the seventies, when it was established in the United States of America as a deliberately diffuse communications device which could sidestep the effects of a nuclear attack by the Soviet Union, was an altogether different phenomenon from the Internet of the eighties, when it was associated primarily with the anti-state ethos of the latterday counterculture, and different again from the commercialized 'fee not free' Internet which did not fully emerge until the mid-nineties.

In attempting to understand the Internet and the culture surrounding it, I have tried to overcome the one-sidedness of most published accounts by rejecting the techno-determinist method by which they have been written. Instead I have approached the Internet and the culture surrounding it as a particular expression of society as a whole. To my mind, the society in which we live now is wholly characterized by its contradictions; and these in turn are clearly expressed at the social frontier which is known as 'cyberculture'.

We live in a social system that for two hundred years has brought larger and larger numbers of people together in the act of making our world, while at the same time pulling them apart and alienating them from each other and from themselves. Moreover, this is a social system which relies on innovation, but finds itself increasingly ill-at-ease with new developments. In the late twentieth century, the contradictions in what Hegel called 'the anti-social society' are more acute than ever before. Cyberculture both reflects and refracts these contradictions, and can best be understood in these terms.

The format of this book takes account of the contemporary fetish for the arbitrary. What could be more arbitrary than attempting to comprehend the information superhighway and the surrounding culture under a series of headings which slavishly follow the letters of the alphabet? On the other hand, the requirement to begin at A and finish at Z goes very much against the contemporary flow; and indeed it is intended as my personal rejoinder to the current hostility towards linearity.

Lastly, I would like to explain why I have used so many references not from the Internet itself, but from printed matter which has been written about cyberspace. This is because I think the expectations of cyberculture are as interesting, and possibly more indicative of society as a whole, than what happens in cyberspace itself. Moreover, in the world of print, there are still people called editors who do an excellent job in weeding out the verbiage and irrelevancies of writers. Editors are often absent from the Internet, which means that online analysis is often inferior to its counterpart offline.

My thanks are due to freelance IT consultant Mark Beachill, who was generous with his advice and expertise. Any errors or misconceptions in the following text are entirely my own.

ANDREW CALCUTT

Anarchy/authority

Cyberspace is regarded as both the end of the state and the extension of state surveillance and control.

'Cyberspace: anarchy in action or Big Brother in waiting?'[1]

This headline from *The Guardian* shows the divergence of opinion on the vexed relationship between the Internet and the state. Some commentators hold that the coming of the Internet spells the end of the state as we know it. Others maintain that the state will take over the Internet and use it as the ultimate surveillance device.

The end-of-the-state thesis enjoys support from individuals who grew up on different sides of the old left–right divide. For the ex-Left, former Situationist and Sex Pistols manager Malcolm McLaren has welcomed the Internet as 'a fantastic anarchic weapon' which threatens to disrupt capitalist society.[2] Meanwhile the libertarian right-winger Ian Angell, professor of information systems at the London School of Economics, also proclaims 'the death of the nation state' at the hands of the 'information revolution':

> A new order (which many will call disorder) is being forced upon an unsuspecting world by advances in telecommunications. Information technology...is changing the whole nature of political governance and its relationship to commerce, and commerce itself...everywhere the nation state is in retreat...citizens are losing their faith in the nation state, seeing it as a peculiarly twentieth-century phenomenon...no nation state has an automatic right to exist.[3]

The notion of the powerless state is not confined to mavericks such as McLaren and Angell. The suggestion that the Information Age will spell the demise of the self-contained nation state connects with the welter of theories, grouped under the label 'globalization', which hold that economic activity is now so globalized that no nation state is big enough to impose an agenda upon it. This is the assumption underlying the proclamations of a new, non-national information culture which have been voiced by mainstream commentators such as Robert Reich, the erstwhile economic adviser to President Bill Clinton, and British media pundit Martin Jacques. 'All that will remain rooted within national borders are the people who comprise a nation', says Reich;[4] while Jacques avers that 'the most dramatic single aspect of the new culture is the end of the nation state'.[5] Even the *Wall Street Journal* has admitted that the 'nature of an information age economy' is inimical to the traditional nation state.[6]

But for every commentator who sees the information revolution as the end of the state, there is another who regards it as the harbinger of Big Brother. For these commentators, the surveillance capacity of digital technologies facilitates the development of a new totalitarianism.

The French commentator Paul Virilio has described the Information Age as 'narco-capitalism', and warns that 'info-tainment' will be as debilitating as narcotic drugs. Noting that the Internet has its origins in a Pentagon communications system designed to resist the effects of nuclear war, he portrays the ascendancy of digital communications as the latest and most virulent incarnation of the military-industrial complex.[7]

Simon Davies, director general of Privacy International, puts an apocalyptic gloss upon Virilio's theories about the 'surveillance society':

> the modern surveillance camera has become truly awesome. Connect it to a moderately priced computer and it can achieve what the Stasi could only dream about... across the Atlantic, the Florida-based Neurometric Company has developed a computerised facial recognition system which can scan a crowd at the rate of 20 faces a second, digitise the faces and match them against identities in a database.[8]

In the UK edition of *Wired*, Davies warned that:

> by 1997...this type of machine will have the capacity to scan a database of 50 million faces. Images from any closed circuit camera can be linked into the system, as long as those images are processed and transmitted in digital form.

Almost the whole population of Britain can now be monitored by a network of cameras linked to a single database. No wonder Davies titled his article 'Welcome home, Big Brother'.

Along similar lines, a number of commentators have remarked upon the transparency of digital communications. 'Our e-mail is like postcards', writes Brent Gregston, a columnist for *Internet* magazine, 'only worse because it can be automatically scanned for subversive keywords *en masse* ...if these developments continue, their enormous surveillance potential will leave individuals' lives vulnerable to an unprecedented concentration of scrutiny and authority'.[9]

In *.net* magazine, veteran commentator Bill Thompson noted that there would be no need to introduce ID cards in cyberspace, because Net-surfers have never had any choice but to disclose their identity:

> You leave digital footprints wherever you step in cyberspace, and it doesn't take an electronic Sherlock Holmes to trace your path. In the real world police forces introduce video surveillance of town centres, car parks and other public areas, but in cyberspace you have never been free from this sort of attention. It *is* possible to pretend to be someone else...but as you journey round the Net, you are carrying the digital equivalent of a neon sign that flashes your home address and phone number...
>
> One of the arguments against the compulsory issuing of identity cards is that we have a legitimate claim to go unremarked. If you want to go to a café, you should not need to account for your decision to the State. As part of that, you should not have to prove your identity in order to be able to exercise this right. On the Internet you are constantly having to 'prove' your identity...Unlike the street, which is held in common by all, every piece of virtual real estate in cyberspace is owned and every owner uses their right to demand identification from visitors.[10]

Thompson recognised that there is no public space online; and that the anonymity associated with public space is equally absent. His observations seem to justify the suggestion that the information superhighway might better be described as a 'snooper-highway'.

Likewise, the Dutch academic Paul Frissen notes that 'bureaucractic surveillance is facilitated on an unknown scale through computer matching, profiling and and all kinds of tracking devices'. Citing Beniger (*The Control Revolution*, Cambridge, Massachusetts, 1986) and Zuurmond (*The Infocracy*, Phaedrus, s-Gravenhage, 1994), Frissen maintains that 'sophisticated bureaucracy enters into a tight coalition with technocratically advanced technology', leading to a new form of social control – 'infocracy':

> Classical limitations to bureaucracy in physical, cognitive, political and societal terms seemingly are overcome... Informatization creates an information architecture which substitutes bureaucratic control and coordination. Instead of a bureaucracy we witness the birth of an 'infocracy'... virtuality does not transform the capitalist system. To some extent it supports it.[11]

Predictions of a global techno-state seem to be the mirror image of the end-of-the-state prophecy. Interestingly, both forecasts can be traced back to the sixties, to the work of media-guru Marshall McLuhan. In *The Global Village*, McLuhan declared that 'the concept of nationalism will fade and regional governments will fall as the political implications of spaceship earth create a world government'.[12]

The end-of-the-state thesis and the notion of the digital techno-state cannot both be correct. But neither of these ideas is entirely wrong. Both theories are fatally flawed; but they can still be useful if we think of them as partial descriptions of broader trends in the re-casting of society and the re-formatting of state power.

The end-of-the-state thesis focuses on the Internet, with particular emphasis on its operation as a de-centred network which can bypass traditional mechanisms of state control. This capacity is often summed in the following soundbites: 'Information wants to be be free' and 'The Net interprets censorship as damage and re-routes itself around it'.

These proverbial phrases (coined, respectively, by Stewart Brand of the Massachusetts Institute of Technology and John Gilmore of the Electronic Frontier Foundation) point towards the replicability of digitized information.

The technical effect of digitization is to extend the replicability of commodities and diminish their particularity. In short, private property can now be converted into a different physical form at the stroke of a keyboard. This facility throws a spanner in the works of property laws and methods of social control which were drafted in a bygone era, at a time when a book was a book and a film was a film, and it took Cecil B. de Mille and a cast of of thousands to turn one into the other.

The problems now facing commodity-owners – and their traditional guarantor, the nation state – were highlighted by Anne W. Branscomb, a Harvard communications lawyer, in a special issue of *Scientific American*:

> The ease with which electronic impulses can be manipulated, modified and erased is hostile to a deliberate legal system that arose in an era of tangible things and relies on documentary evidence to validate transactions, incriminate miscreants and affirm contractual relations. What have been traditionally known as letters, journals, photographs, conversations, videotapes, and audiotapes merge into a single stream of undifferentiated electronic impulses.[13]

Digitization is the most recent instance of capitalist commodity production tending to overcome its own limitations. In its role as the guarantor of private property, the capitalist nation state has been struggling to come to terms with the novel and apparently subversive properties of digitized commodities. As we have seen, these technical properties have led numerous commentators to suggest that the state will no longer be able to operate as the guarantor of commodity-producing societies. But this is to underestimate the capacity of the state to reformulate itself in accordance with technical developments in commodity production. Great strides in this direction have already been made, as Branscomb went on to point out:

> Cyberspace is a frontier where territorial rights are being established and electronic environments are being differentiated in much the same way as the Western frontier was pushed back by voyageurs, pioneers, miners and cattlemen. And the entrepreneurs are arriving with their new

institutions... the common law of cyberspace evolve[s] as users express their concerns and seek consensual solutions to common problems.[14]

Financial Times columnist John Kay was more succinct: 'the development of new information technologies is changing much of our lives. But it does not change the basic laws of business and economics.'[15]

Reports of the death of the capitalist state have been exaggerated. Property relations are not being overturned, but in the context of digital communications their legal form is subject to modification. The same is true of the guarantor of property relations, the state, which is currently undergoing a process of renewal. Moreover, the modification of the state has been under way since the seventies – before the advent of digital communications. The development of, say, the Internet has reinforced already-existing pressures for worn-out state institutions to reformulate themselves; but it is not the original author of this dynamic. Indeed, the character of the Information Age has itself been rewritten by the same broad social trends which have prompted the reformulation of traditional institutions.

The Information Age was first talked about nearly 40 years ago, at which time it was envisaged as the apogee of state-sponsored centralization. In the Swinging London of the 1960s, for example, information technology was symbolized by the Post Office Tower – a monument to centralization and state intervention. In the early nineties, London's first Internet café, Cyberia, was established in the shadow of the tower, now renamed the BT Tower. Cyberia, and its application of the Internet, are indicative of a society which is diffuse, privatised and individuated. The contrast between IT in the sixties and IT in the nineties suggests that the Information Age is not an autonomous agent which dominates society and its institutions; rather it has shifted in accordance with the changing mood of the times. Instead of ascribing an independent momentum to the 'Information Age', it would be more instructive to examine the successive manifestations of information technology as changing reflections of the overarching social contexts in which they developed.

To recapitulate: the end-of-the-state thesis overlooks the reformulation of the state; and it fails to locate the development and implementation of digital technology in the overarching social context of the day. However, if we look at this thesis critically, we can find a use for it as a reflection of one of the trends operating in society today, namely the demise of the the traditional, outdated forms of the state.

Likewise, the notion of the techno-state is a reflection of a real trend, namely the increase in state power over individuals in society. But it is just as one-sided as the end-of-the-state thesis.

Whereas the end-of-the-state thesis recognizes that some forms of state power are now out of date, and from this recognition draws the false conclusion that the state is therefore doomed, the Big Brother thesis recognizes that the state is accruing new powers, but tries to fit this trend into the equally outdated model of the totalitarian state.

Advocates of the Big Brother thesis tend to endow the state with far more coherence than it can currently muster. They extrapolate their notions of the future state from previous incarnations of state power (fascism, for example) in which state institutions were more centralized and less fragmented than they are today.

Simon Davies, in his book *Big Brother*,[16] seemed to envisage the techno-state as a singular, all-seeing eye with the capacity to incorporate each citizen's every move into its unstinting, fully integrated gaze. Technically speaking, this is a possibility. But the lack of confidence and the low level of coordination among those in authority today mean that they are in no position to use this technical potential to the full. Even if technology has improved surveillance capabilities, a nation state such as the United Kingdom, which can no longer generate Big Ideas and which experiences increasing difficulty in maintaining a coherent image of itself, is hardly likely to succeed in mapping a big picture of all its inhabitants.

So, the Big Brother thesis reflects the extension of state power; but also refracts this process through the distorting mirror of an outdated totalitarian model. Like the end-of-the-state thesis, it is a one-sided expression of current trends.

Both theories attempt to compress contemporary developments into the models of the past. Furthermore, they both tend towards techno-determinism. That is to say, they assume that technology can be the primary determinant of social trends. In this respect they follow the muddle-headed approach of Marshall McLuhan, who claimed that the Great Crash of 1929 was caused by the advent of jazz and the radio.

If we stop expecting time to stand still, and if we remember to locate the development of digital communications within the overall flow of society, the reality of the increasingly close relationship between the state and the Information Age starts to reveal itself. One of the most significant aspects of this emerging relationship is the extent to which the Information Age, and the Internet in particular, has come to symbolize the process of reformatting the state and abandoning previous modes of exercising power.

In Britain, New Labour exemplifies the end of the old state; and, in turn, New Labour's connection to the Internet exemplifies the party's newness and its abandonment of labour movement traditions. Furthermore, New Labour politicians have seized upon the construction of the information superhighway and tried to make it their own. At a time of deep disillusion with central government and politics in general, the idea that the state will facilitate the construction of the i-way provides a much-needed justification for the continued existence of the governing elite.

Robin Cook is currently serving as Foreign Secretary in Tony Blair's cabinet. While the Conservatives were still in power, Cook had the job of shadowing the Tory Secretary of State for National Heritage; and during this period he mapped out a role for the state as a protagonist in the information revolution. 'There is a new role for the state', Cook wrote, 'in establishing the telecommunications infrastructure on which the information revolution depends'.[17]

Moreover, Cook stressed that New Labour's new role in the information revolution would require the abandonment of an earlier mode of government and the development of a new regulatory model: 'state regulation may be a more appropriate response to the new industrial process, rather than state ownership...state ownership of information or knowledge is both unattainable and undesirable'.

Cook went on to suggest that by managing the information revolution the state would validate itself; he also suggested that only 'the left' could carry out this role satisfactorily:

> Only the left can offer an ideology that validates the role of the state in ensuring the infrastructure that provides universal access, and in regulating it to guarantee the free flow of information across the system.

Cook's notion of a 'free flow' which is guaranteed by state regulation is a conundrum which Big Brother might be proud of (the notion of a revolution guaranteed by those already in authority is equally contradictory). But his role model was not Big Brother so much as Al Gore, Vice-President of the United States of America and the frontman for Washington's role in the construction of the information superhighway. Gore had already set out his stall as the uber-guarantor of universal access to the new mobility of the Information Age:

> It will be up to the federal and state policymakers to determine how best to build a universal, high-speed network, to reconcile the competing corporate interests and to create a network that maximises the benefits enjoyed by all Americans.[18]

It is ironic that while post-national globalization theories have become the new orthodoxy in some government departments, in neighbouring offices the nation state has been nominated, and to some extent rehabilitated, as the architect of the 'i-way'.

Back in Britain, the revelation that 'Blair aims to "do a Kennedy" on the Internet' emphasized New Labour's eagerness to harness the Internet and incorporate it into a new image of statecraft. The *Sunday Times* reported that:

> Tony Blair, like two of the American presidents he most admires, is turning to technology to strengthen his bond with those who elected him. He is considering using the Internet for a global version of question time in which he would be challenged directly by members of the public. The prime minister's advisers want him to 'capture' the Internet and make it 'his' medium, just as John Kennedy

manipulated television to become the first political star of the small screen and Franklin D. Roosevelt's reassuring voice made his name synonymous with radio.[19]

The *Sunday Times* story shows New Labour attempting to use the Internet as the means to enhance its image and to reconnect senior politicians with the people. As such, it epitomizes the real character of the emerging relationship between the Internet and the state in an age of disconnection and estrangement from traditional institutions.

Boys/girls

The Internet is heralded as the premier domain of a new woman-friendly mode of existence, and simultaneously attacked for being the last resort of the unreconstructed male.

The masculine has associated itself with centralised control, and women and machines have had to function through the top controlling function of the male. We're moving away from that to a creeping, growing from the bottom, grassroots network notion, which itself is a feminist notion, of women organising themselves away from those top-down power structures.

Cyberfeminist Sadie Plant, quoted in 'Deadlier than the e-mail', Linda Grant, *The Guardian*, 30 November 1994.

[The Internet] has no organising core, but pulls itself together from the bottom-up, replicating networks and making connections, just as women have organised themselves.

Sadie Plant, 'Babes in The Net', *New Statesman and Society*, 27 February 1995.

At the moment online it looks like a men's changing room at a football match. There are all these men standing there at the door saying 'you can come in if you want to, and you can take it'. You'd be bloody stupid as a woman to go in there. You're not physically barring people, but the sense of it being pissed-on male territory is obvious.

Australian feminist Dale Spender, quoted in Jim McClellan's column in the Life section, *The Observer*, 29 October 1995.

It's a pissing contest.

IT consultant Lisa Kimball, quoted in 'Men, Women and Computers: the gender gap in high tech', *Newsweek*, 16 May 1994.

The gender of cyberspace is in dispute. On the one hand, the non-hierarchichal, de-centred Internet has been welcomed

11

by cyberfeminists as a step beyond the 'phallic principles' of
traditional power structures. They maintain that the digital
revolution is spontaneously re-engineering the social conditions in which patriarchy has thrived up to now. In the words
of Sadie Plant, 'women will have the last laugh in cyberspace'.[1]

On the other hand, cyberspace is widely associated with
pornography, harassment and the rancid odour of rampant
males. Robin Hunt's story for *The Guardian* about online
celebrity nude sites ('Internet anoraks on-line to become
dirty mac brigade at touch of button') played on these
expectations of cyberspace. Describing the culture surrounding such sites, Hunt wrote: 'It is a cross between train-
spotting, reading *Hello!* magazine and collecting football
stickers of Premier League stars...a defining trend of the
Loaded nineties.' He succeeded in conjuring up an image of
the Internet as simultaneously nerdish and macho.[2]

Along similar lines, *Newsweek* ran a special feature entitled
'Men Women and Computers: the gender gap in high tech', in
which the magazine's senior writer Barbara Kantrowitz criticized the computer industry for being heavily male-dominated:
'Computer culture is created, controlled and defined by men.
Women are often as welcome as a system crash...it's that
male-machine bonding thing...They don't call it Game-*Boy*
for nothing.'[3] George Hackett, another *Newsweek* staff writer,
joked about what men and women want from computers:
'What do women want? Who knows? What do men want?
Something bigger, cooler and faster than yours.'

The contradictory expectations of cyberspace (woman-
friendly/male-dominated) have given rise to the further
expectation of a sex war in cyberspace. To illustrate the
conflict between the mutually exclusive expectations of men
and women, a cartoon in the *Newsweek* feature juxtaposed a
woman saying 'My friends and I are teaching dolphins to
communicate through e-mail', with a man who declared 'I
like to blow stuff up'.

The sex war in cyberspace even has its own computer
game, *Gender Wars*, which, according to the games reviewer
in the *Daily Telegraph*'s Connected supplement, 'is set in a
futuristic society in which the relationship between the
sexes has degenerated into full-scale warfare'.[4]

There are signs, however, that the extent of the sex war in cyberspace has been greatly exaggerated. In the summer of 1996, the *Financial Times* suggested that 'women are floating into cyberspace in increasing numbers'. The author of the piece, Victoria Griffith, reported that 'a year ago most studies estimated that only 15 per cent of Net users were women. Today, surveys place the figure at closer to 40 per cent.' Paul Sagan, editor of new media at Time Warner, was quoted as saying that 'when this first started, it was something guys created for guys. Now the digital world is starting to look like the analogue world.'

Griffith went on to point out that 'while many observers strongly believe the gender lines in cyberspace are clearly marked, others feel the differences are exaggerated'. In support of the second supposition, she quoted Hunter Madson of Hotwired, the online section of *Wired* magazine, who said: 'I think men and women are basically looking for the same thing. Making sites easy to navigate, helping users save time and money...those are things companies should do to attract men and women.'[5]

If Madson is correct, and cyberspace is not, after all, divided along gender lines, this would suggest that the sex war in cyberspace has been phoney all along. But why wage a phoney war in the one arena of social intercourse where no one can tell what sex you are? One possible explanation is that the protagonists in the phoney war have an interest in play-acting their respective gender roles. This would be in keeping with current trends in wider society.

In Britain the runaway success of the magazine *Loaded* (strapline: For men who should know better) exemplifies the development of phoney masculinity. A new generation of young men, for whom the traditional role of sole bread-winner is no longer available, lack the confidence to lord it over their own families. Unnerved by recent changes in the labour market, they compensate by adopting a lifestyle in which their masculinity is knowingly overplayed. 'New Lad' and 'Lad-ism' are the labels which journalists have attached to their ironic overacting. *Loaded* (incidentally, the first British style magazine to carry a regular column about the Internet) is the publication which made its reputation by living out these labels to the letter.

Whereas in previous generations male machismo may have been a reflection of bullish self-confidence, Lad-ism, by contrast, is a faltering attempt to offset the unprecedented effects of what has become known as 'the crisis of masculinity'. While winking at the girls, it seems the Lads are really nodding at their own insecurities.

In this context, one of the attractions of the Internet is that beleaguered males can retreat into it, just as they take refuge in the overblown images of masculinity on the pages of *Loaded*. In the virtual world, on Internet sites where the smell of the locker room is pungent, they can play at being 'real men' without fear of being caught out by embarrassing, actually existing social trends such as the relative feminization of the workplace. 'Cyberjocks', as they are sometimes called, are thus identifying with a caricature of masculinity in the hope that this will compensate them for the perceived decline in 'male power'.

The tragedy (if that is not too grand a word) of their performance is that play-acting of this sort can only draw attention to the very qualities in which the Lads of today are so sadly lacking. Overacting the role of the bullish male only emphasizes the insecurities which such role-playing may have been intended to obscure.

Lad-ism and phoney masculinity are fairly well documented. The self-caricature inherent in contemporary feminism is a less familiar phenomenon. But this is precisely the role which cyberfeminism seems to be playing.

In its original incarnation in the seventies, feminism – or the women's movement, as it came to be known – sought to acquire more power for women. In Oxford in 1970, the founding conference of the women's movement called for free abortion on demand, free 24-hour nursery care, and free and safe contraception – demands which were designed to uncouple women from a life of domesticity and put them on a par with men. The original aim of the movement was for women to become more like men, especially in the exercise of power. But womanhood proved an unsatisfactory basis for the project of liberation, and throughout the late seventies and eighties, the women's movement became less coherent and more fragmented.

As the quest for power through sisterhood became less plausible, so the sisters came to the conclusion that power itself is suspect, undesirable and even un-sisterly. This trend seems to have reached its apogee in cyberfeminism and the attempt to translate powerlessness into the defining characteristic of a new mode of existence. In cyberfeminism, the reality of women's exclusion from the centres of power in society has been transposed into the fantasy that the Internet is 'beyond outdated power structures'. It is a phoney feminism from which the laudable aspirations of the power-hungry women's movement have been stripped away.

Just as Lad-ism represents a retreat from the 'crisis of masculinity', so cyberfeminism responds to the failure of feminism by retreating into a new place – cyberspace – where accepting a life without power can be redefined as living 'beyond hierarchy'.

Likewise, cyberfeminists tend to assume that the dynamic of digital communications towards a more woman-friendly mode of existence will run its course automatically, without any effort or intervention on their part. It is surely no coincidence that the fantasy of going with the flow towards a muted sort of liberation has arisen at a time when the ideas and politics with which to go against the flow are sadly lacking. Indeed the timing would suggest that the notion of automatic quasi-liberation has come about as a way of coming to terms with the exhaustion of feminist politics.

The cyberjocks and cyberfeminists in the phoney sex war seem to have a lot in common. Both groups are play-acting; and both are also able to see through their own fragile performances. They fall back on irony as a prophylactic sheath which protects them against their self-consciousness as well as their insecurities.

The seminal text of cyberfeminism is 'The Cyborg Manifesto', written towards the end of the eighties by Donna J. Haraway, who is professor of the history of consciousness at the University of California. Haraway's thesis is that the interaction between human beings and technology can no longer be described as a relationship between *man* (my emphasis) and machines. Increasingly, this interaction is moving in a woman-friendly direction, to the point where its personification in the idea of the cyborg (half-human, half-machine) is taking on feminine rather than masculine characteristics. The future, in other words, is female.

But Haraway's essay was not only about human beings, gender and technology; it was also an exploration of the shrinking social space available to those who might still refer to themselves as 'socialist feminists', at a time when both socialism and feminism were already past their sell-by date.

Haraway must have been thinking about her own political position when, in the text of 'The Cyborg Manifesto', she described it as 'an effort to build an ironic political myth'. Furthermore, she defined irony as being not only 'about humour and serious play', but also as 'a rhetorical strategy and a political method' which she 'would like to see more honoured in socialist feminism'.[6]

The essay seems to express Haraway's desire to continue seeing herself as a political animal. But, at the same time, she no longer feels she can commit herself to a single, political outlook. Indeed she has accepted the postmodern, post-political notion that 'the production of universal, totalising theory is a major mistake'. As a post-feminist, she describes this 'mistake' as 'phallogocentrism'.

Of course there is a terrible contradiction between wanting to be politically committed, but finding oneself in a historical context where there is nothing in politics that seems to merit total commitment. In order to resolve this contradiction, albeit artificially, Haraway invokes a *deus ex machina* in the form of irony. The irony in her 'political myth' allows her to keep the faith while at the same time extricating herself from its failure.

Haraway's 'ironic' faith in feminism allows her to believe/ unbelieve at one and the same time. This is a sad reflection on a generation of radicals who have lost confidence in their ability to change society, or even to understand it as a totality – yet who cannot bear the thought of themselves as mere spectators whose relationship to the world is purely passive.

Ironic cyberfeminism is the mirror-image of the ironic masculinity practised by cyberjocks. The Lads on-line cannot picture themselves changing the world – unlike their fathers and grandfathers, who may never have achieved anything so grand but whose self-image remained unshakeably bound up with notions of agency and purposive activity.

The Lads of today cannot bear to tear up the traditional image of the heroic male. The conundrum they face is that they cannot live up to this image; but neither can they live it down. Their equivalent of Haraway's 'ironic political myth' is their ironized version of masculinity. Hence the tendency to act out a pantomime version of the heroic male which is ironic in that it is simultaneously a compensation for powerlessness and an acknowledgement of impotence in society.

Cyberjocks are clinging on to an exaggerated idea of how 'real men' used to be. But they themselves do not believe that a return to the past is possible. Meanwhile, cyberfeminists take their inspiration from a mythical notion of the female future. But they themselves do not believe that feminist ideas, or any other form of politics, can make the future happen. Both groups have conceded that the future is whatever it turns out to be. In the words of the song, 'Que sera sera'. Their respective pantomime performances are caricatures of human agency which have been prompted by the increasingly widespread assumption – in cyberculture and beyond – that nothing much can be done.

In this respect, the phoney sex war in cyberspace is a fantastic reflection of real changes in society. Ours is an age which has rejected the hero in favour of the victim, and any man who makes the mistake of trying to play the hero is likely to be accused of 'maladaptive masculinity'.

Appropriately enough, the anti-heroic mood has found an expression in the way that computers and the Internet are currently being sold to the general public: as an educational tool for children, as a pathway to community and local identity, and as a tool which can help women and men juggle careers with their role as carers; but never as an instrument for mastering nature. Indeed the figure of the masterful male appears only as the butt of jokes, as in the spring 1995 campaign for Microsoft in which the hunky young man stands corrected by a child of primary school age, or in an ironic capacity, as in the summer 1996 advertisement for Apple computers which was a pastiche of the film *Mission Impossible* (itself a parody of the television series from the seventies).

In the selling of cyberspace, what is being advertised is not the potential for socializing the domestic environment, but the extent to which the external world – society – is being domesticated. This is the first time since the industrial revolution that a new generation of technology has been presented, not as an instrument of (male) mastery, but as something more akin to a lifestyle-enhancing fitted kitchen.

This trend in computer advertising is one of many indications that, underneath the phoney sex war in cyberspace, a real attack on the 'maladaptive' idea of human beings as heroes is currently taking place.

Community/alienation

Some commentators champion cyberspace as the home of 'virtual communities'; others warn that it is a place of extreme alienation.

The best-known advocate of online community is Howard Rheingold, whose book *Virtual Communities* documents his experience of the WELL (Whole Earth 'Lectronic Link), a San Francisco-based computer-mediated community which began as an offshoot of the ecologically conscious magazine, the *Whole Earth Catalog*. Rheingold welcomes communities like the WELL as a partial replacement for the traditional public spaces which are now lost to American society.

In the introduction to *Virtual Communities*, Rheingold describes how he discovered a sense of togetherness and cooperation online:

> Since the summer of 1985, for an average of two hours a day, seven days a week, I've been plugging my personal computer into my telephone and making contact with the WELL (Whole Earth 'Lectronic Link) – a computer conferencing system that enables people around the world to carry on public conversations and exchange private electronic mail (e-mail). The idea of a community accessible only via my computer screen sounded cold to me at first, but I learned quickly that people can feel passionately about e-mail and computer conferences. I've become one of them. I care about these people I met through my computer, and I care deeply about the future of the medium that enables us to assemble...
>
> The virtual village of a few hundred people which I stumbled upon in 1985 grew to eight thousand by 1993. It became clear to me during the first few months of that history that I was participating in the self-design of a new kind of culture. I watched the community's social contracts stretch and change as the people who discovered and started building the WELL in its first year or two were joined by so many others. Norms were established,

challenged, changed, re-established, rechallenged, in a
kind of speeded-up social evolution...

People in virtual communities do just about everything
people do in real life, but we leave our bodies behind. You
can't kiss anybody and nobody can punch you in the nose,
but a lot can happen within those boundaries. To the millions
who have been drawn into it, the richness and vitality of
computer-linked cultures is attractive, even addictive.[1]

Rheingold entered cyberculture via the counterculture and
its aftermath on the West Coast of America. Cristina Odone
came to it by way of the *Catholic Herald*, but she has advocated
virtual communities in terms which are remarkably similar to
Rheingold's:

Just as the moral fabric of our social connections seems
to be irredeemably tattered, the Internet pulls us into
têtes-à-têtes that enlarge our sense of reality to encompass
'others' – from stranger to neighbour. Like an unfolding
epistolary novel that chronicles our history, the messages
(wordy, idiosyncratic, persuasive, or desperate) fill our
computer screen, impossible to ignore, and they bring us
face-to-face with other people's concerns.

These connections – so haphazard and spontaneous –
seem to rekindle that elusive sense of belonging that lies
at the core of the traditional community... the Web could
serve as the first building block in the creation of a whole
new social solidarity, founded upon cross-cultural, interdisciplinary dialogues and cemented in an 'empowerment'
and 'enfranchisement' of marginalised individuals.

A brave new world where heart and soul are restored to
the body politic by giving voice to the voiceless and public
space to the individual.[2]

Meanwhile, other commentators have looked into cyberculture and seen alienation, not community. At a conference
entitled Culture, Technology and Creativity, hosted by the
Institute of Contemporary Arts in London on 6 April 1991,
Kevin Robins described cyberculture as a new way of shut-
ting oneself off from physical reality:

More escapist than about changing social reality, there is
a negative agenda in the way new technologies are

perceived. There is the desire to rise above reality, as if we've been living as caterpillars and new tech will turn us into butterflies. The notion of liberation is to be free from reality... to live in a microworld, small, independent, based on the interaction between the person and computer system within a defined set of rules.[3]

Writing in a similar vein, in *The Guardian*, the distinguished academic John Gray dismissed 'virtual communities' as 'a designer Utopia, customised for people who believe in technical fixes and not in morality or politics'.[4]

Likewise, in 'Reading *Mondo 2000*', an essay on the ethos of the eponymous West Coast, New Edge magazine which appeared in *Flame Wars: The Discourse of Cyberculture*, Vivian Sobchack dissected the cyberculturists' enthusiasm for 'getting rid of the meat', and detected disdain for the 'imperfect human body' and estrangement from 'the imperfect world':

M2's [*Mondo 2000*'s] supposedly utopian celebration of the liberating possibilities of the new electronic frontier promotes an ecstatic dream of disembodiment. This is alienation raised to the level of ekstasis: 'A being out of its place.' It is also an apolitical fantasy of escape. Historical accounts of virtual reality tell us that one of the project's initial slogans was 'Reality isn't enough anymore', but psychoanalytic accounts would more likely tell us that the slogan should be read in its inverse form – that is 'Reality is too much right now'.[5]

The celebration of alienation in cyberculture would explain why mirrored sunglasses – the fashion accessory which, along with the black leather jacket, symbolizes estrangement from the rest of the world – were a recurring motif among the novelists and short story writers who later became known as 'cyberpunks'. In the preface to *Mirrorshades*, the first cyberpunk anthology, the novelist and essayist Bruce Sterling noted that 'preferably in chrome and matte black', mirrored sunglasses were 'the Movement's totem colors' which 'appeared in story after story, as a kind of literary badge'.[6]

How can cyberspace be at one and the same time the home of new communities and a place where alienation is

celebrated to the point of 'ekstasis'? Sobchack's approach of
reading the slogans of cyberculture in their 'inverse form'
provides some insight into this contradictory co-existence.

Cyber-communitarians are enthusiastic about the new
forms of conversation facilitated by digital commmunications.
But the new community is perhaps more remarkable for
what it excludes than for what is included in it.

'E-mail is not a good way to get angry at someone, because
you can't interact.'[7] This is how Bill Gates summed up the
limitations inherent in e-mail. But perhaps the limited character of e-mail is also what makes it attractive. On the Internet, the immediacy and unpredictability of interpersonal
communications are reduced to a manageable level by the
mediating role of the computer. The unpleasant possibilities
of face-to-face exchanges – not having enough time to formulate a reply, the remote possiblity that a physical fight
might ensue – are simply absent (recalling Rheingold's observation in the introduction to *Virtual Communities*, discussed
earlier in this section, that online 'nobody can punch you in
the nose'[8]). The result is a form of communication which in
the very moment of transcending geographical limitations
also imposes new restrictions which are often a source of
comfort to the frightened interlocutors of today.

In other words, e-mail is a form of communication which is
appropriate to a historical context in which many individuals
feel peculiarly alienated and at risk from each other. In this
respect, the desire for virtual communities is partly a desire to
alienate oneself further from a society from which one already
feels alienated. The community functions in this instance as a
safe haven which shuts out the wider world and its apparently
intractable problems.

Ziauddin Sardar, co-editor of a special edition of *futures*
journal entitled 'Cyberspace: To Boldly Go', made some per-
tinent distinctions between 'real' and 'cyberspace communities', before going on to point out that the latter often
operate as an escape route from the former:

> Real community creates context. It generates issues which
> arise with relations to time and space, history and contem-
> porary circumstances, and require responsible judgement
> – which is why so many issues are difficult, they require

balancing of opposing pressures. A cyberspace community is self-selecting, exactly what a real community is not; it is contingent and transient, depending on the shared interest of those with the attention span of a 30-second sound bite. The essence of real community is its presumptive perpetuity – you have to worry about other people because they will always be there. In a cyberspace community you can shut people off at the click of a mouse and go elsewhere. One therefore has no responsibility of any kind... cyberspace provides an easy simulation for the sweaty hard work required for building real communities. But virtual communities serve another purpose: they protect from the race and gender mix of real community, from the contamination of pluralism.[9]

Sardar has touched on another sense in which cyber-communitarianism is not antithetical to alienation. Besides *what* is left out from the comparatively narrow bandwidth of online communication, virtual communities also define themselves according to *who* is excluded. Online and off, the coming together of a self-selecting minority occurs in the same moment as the all-important exclusion of others. The preference for involvement in a particular community, digital or otherwise, is again connected to the abandonment of society as a whole. The online community is essentially a club which represents a retreat from the street and other public thoroughfares.

This dynamic is clearly visible in the advent of online home schooling. In wired cities small but growing numbers of children are logging on to lessons in cyberspace. In 1994 *Newsweek* reported that 'once the primary domain of either fundamentalist Christians or free-to-be hippies, home schooling is beginning to appeal to middle class families searching for safe havens'. Referring to a 'virtual school' based in Seattle, the *Newsweek* article pointed out that pioneer families are paying $4500 per child in tuition fees so as to avoid the 'common threat' of 'fear of public-school violence, mediocrity and unforgiving bureaucracies'.[10]

In previous generations the middle classes saw it as their role to educate the rest of society. But nowadays they are increasingly alienated from a world which has ignored their best efforts and seems to prefer to dumb-down. In this context, online education serves as a means of escaping from the Herculean tasks for which a less alienated middle class would previously have taken responsibility.

'Camwatch' is another example of the formation of an online community through the process of excluding others. In March 1994, *Computer Shopper* magazine carried an article about 'the new computer network that's helping to fight crime in Cambridgeshire'. Reporter Graeme Kidd described how Chief Inspector Paul Styles established a 'telecommunity' of Neighbourhood Watch members and police officers: 'Camwatch, the first e-mail system in the country to link serving officers and members of the public, has already led to arrests and helped develop a stronger sense of community in the villages it serves.'[11]

Nick Mair, described as 'a computer owner who is a member of a Neighbourhood Watch scheme', explained how the Camwatch bulletin board was used to alert local residents to the unwelcome presence of 'a group of Geordies' who were 'offering to take orders for fresh fish' but appeared to be 'more interested in looking into my house over my shoulder than they were in selling me fish' – that is, they seemed to be casing the joint. Mair boasted that, with the help of Camwatch, 'the whole village was tuned in to the arrival of these suspicious characters', and 'hopefully these characters got a clear message to leave our village alone'.

Reading his comments in their 'inverse form', as Sobchack recommends, one might suggest that the village was made 'whole' – became a community – in the act of excluding the 'group of Geordies' and demanding that they should 'leave our village alone' – an act of communitarian exclusion which in this instance was facilitated by computer-mediated conferencing.

Even Rheingold's WELL is not immune from such tendencies. When Rheingold describes the members of his virtual community getting together for a non-virtual picnic, the narrow range of their social backgrounds becomes apparent; and the homeboys from the wrong side of the San Francisco Bay are noticeable by their absence. Furthermore, a couple of years after Rheingold published *Virtual Communities*, there was an exodus of original members from the WELL. They decided that their virtual community was oversubscribed, and just as previous generations had taken part in the 'white flight' from inner cities to the suburbs, so they exited from the WELL and took up residence in a new 'cyber-suburb' known as the River.

In an article entitled 'Flight to the Cyber-Suburbs', stephen Graham described the virtual community as 'an electronic antidote to the depressing reality of contemporary urban life'. The Internet, he added, 'allows its dominant users – middle class, suburban Americans – to keep in touch with carefully screened groups of similar people, right across the world, from the safety of their increasingly fortified homes'.[12] In cyberculture, therefore, community and alienation are mutually dependent rather than mutually exclusive, in that the tie that binds the cyber-communitarians together is their alienation from the rest of the world.

However, the exclusion of others does not in itself negate the original desire to build a community. But what kind of community? In 'Netsurfers', an article on the WELL for the Life supplement published by *The Observer*, Jim McClellan described a confessional culture which sounds like an online version of TV's *Oprah*:

> Showing me around the downbeat WELL office is Sausa-lito, California, [Gail] Williams [the system's general manager] explains that when the system first started, the organisers set up a conference called True Confessions designed to encourage people to open up and get personal on-line. They soon found that people didn't need any encouraging. Perhaps it's the result of a kind of liberating ambiguity inherent in on-line communication, which is suspended between speech and writing, between a letter and a phone call, but once on-line, some people can start talking with an honesty and intimacy that's rare in RL (Net slang for Real Life). Currently, the most popular new conference on the WELL is Life Stories, in which WELL beings log on and wax autobiographical.[13]

The prevalence of autobiographical, confessional pieces in both print and broadcasting media shows that their popularity has nothing to do with the hybrid quality of online communication, as McClellan describes it. Rather, it suggests that online and off there is a widespread attempt to create a sense

of communal like-mindedness through sharing the experience of suffering. But the experience of suffering is no basis
on which to build a dynamic sense of community: ultimately,
it can only add to our sense of alienation. This much was
indicated by the response to the sudden death of Princess
Diana in a car accident in the late summer of 1997.

In *Internet* magazine, Gail Robinson reported that 'from
personal home pages through to the sites of CNN and the
BBC there was little on the Net that was untouched by
Diana's death'.[14] Meanwhile on the day of Princess Diana's
funeral, hundreds of thousands of people came on to the
streets of London to pay their respects. Across Britain, millions more watched the television coverage. They all wanted
to be part of something, and in a speech given a few days
later, Prime Minister Tony Blair observed that the 'country'
was 'united in grief'.[15] And yet, as the crowds dispersed and
the television stations returned to something like their normal schedules, there was a sense of anti-climax and unfulfil-
ment which was as profound as the communal yearning
which preceded it.

On that day, the British public tried to come together
around the shared experience of suffering. People wanted
to be touched, spiritually, by Princess Diana, who had been
touched by many other sufferers (Aids patients, victims of
land mines) before being touched herself by the cruel hand
of fate. They hoped to be united in this experience, and
thereby to overcome their alienation. But there can be no
such thing as a community of fellow sufferers. A sense of
community can only be derived from activity, and to define
ourselves as fellow sufferers, as the crowds and the television
viewers did on 4 September 1997, is to define ourselves not
as doers but as people to whom things are done, and for
whom the world is a closed book. This is, in fact, tantamount
to alienation; and the events of that day became a reprise of
our alienation rather than its transcendence.

The same sort of impasse is discernible in the coexistence
of community and alienation in cyberculture. Hundreds of
thousands of people have tried to come together in virtual
communities, but the primary experience which they wish to
share is that of the sufferer or victim. They offer an image of
themselves which is defined by passivity (of being done to)

rather than activity (of doing); and it turns out that the attribute upon which they wish to build a community is in fact their own alienation. Thus the powerful aspiration to build communities online only adds to the even more powerful dynamic of alienation in cyberculture and throughout contemporary society.

Democracy/diversity

The Internet is widely expected both to enhance democracy and to facilitate diversity. But democracy and diversity are more contradictory than complementary.

'Digital technology...offers a new democracy dominated neither by the vested interests of political parties nor the mob's baying howl.'[1] In their 'Manifesto For A Digital Society', this was how the editors of *Wired* (UK) summed up the promise of digital democracy. The manifesto was published in what turned out to be the penultimate issue of the UK edition of *Wired*; but the expectation of digital democracy had already been laid out in the first issue of the UK edition, with a front cover which likened the radical eighteenth-century democrat Thomas Paine to a 'digital revolutionary', and a centre spread in which Jon Katz explained why Paine's 'clarion call' for democracy is entirely in keeping with the 'age of information':

> The Net offers what Paine and his revolutionary colleagues hoped for in their own new media – a vast, diverse, passionate, global means of transmitting ideas and opening minds ...If Paine's vision was aborted by the new technologies of the last century, newer technology has brought his vision full circle. If his values no longer have much relevance for conventional journalism, they fit the Net like a glove.[2]

Howard Rheingold has also proffered the opinion that, although the mass media may have become inimical to democracy, the 'many-to-many' medium of the Internet may well contribute to its re-invigoration:

> The mass media, particularly television, changed the mode of discourse among citizens in a way that did not help democracy. The public sphere became a commodity that could be bought and sold. Reasoned argument lost ground to riveting images and emotional sound-bites. Citizens started communicating with each other less as the

advertising industry learnt how to package and market issues and candidates.

As long as electronic networks are accessible to the entire population, affordable, easy to use, and legally protected as a forum for free speech, they have the potential to revitalise the public sphere.[3]

Like Rheingold and the *Wired* school of writers, the Electronic Frontier Foundation (EFF) has advocated a new kind of democratic post-politics to match the new terrain of cyberspace. Internet-style democracy, says EFF board member Esther Dyson, might not need traditional political parties but would 'enable people to organise *ad hoc*, rather than get stuck in some rigid group'.[4]

Recently, however, the EFF has been working alongside the Clinton administration in Washington, presumably in the belief that there can be some kind of convergence between existing political institutions and the new-style cyber-democracy. Although Dyson says she is 'scared they're going to turn into the people they've replaced', she clearly believes that there is some common ground between top-level New Democrats and the ex-hippie counterculture-types who have furnished the EFF with its defining ethos: 'it's very exciting to realise that these are a bunch of people from our generation. In quotes, they "get it".'[5]

However, various commentators have interrogated the notion of cyberdemocracy, pointing out that no technology, in and of itself, can be said to be democratic. After all, both Thomas Paine's *Rights of Man* and Adolf Hitler's *Mein Kampf* entered the public domain by means of the same communications technology – printing. Rheingold himself quotes James Carey on the misleading 'rhetoric of the "technological sublime"' in which technology is invested with autonomous powers and expected to solve social problems by itself:

Despite the manifest failure of technology to resolve pressing issues over the last century, contemporary intellectuals continue to see revolutionary potential in the latest technological gadgets that are pictured as a force outside history and politics.[6]

Rheingold goes on to warn that 'the great weakness of the idea of electronic democracy is that it can be more easily commodified than explained...The Net that is a marvellous lateral network can also be used as a kind of invisible yet inescapable cage.'[7]

Rheingold's concerns, grouped together under the chapter heading 'Disinformocracy', demonstrate that the idea of cyberdemocracy is by no means straightforward. In fact it is riven with contradictions. This is because the attempt to invest neutral technology with an essentially democratic character is currently exposed to counter-trends in which the social application of the same technology turns out to be anti-democratic.

Among cybercitizens the idea of diversity is as popular as the notion of democracy. There is an expectation that cyberspace will provide the places for different peoples to be themselves. The de-centred Internet is held to be particularly appropriate for the expression and realization of many different identities. Cyberspace seems like the ideal location for the emergence of a new civil society in which centrism and uniformity are replaced by the particular and the diverse.

This discourse tends to assume that diversity is essentially subversive. Thus the organizers of a conference at the National Film Theatre in London entitled Forty Acres And A Microchip (a punning reference to the name of black film director Spike Lee's production company, Forty Acres And A Mule, which is itself a reference to the promise of land made to slaves in the USA at the time of their emancipation) sought to challenge what they described as 'the present monocultural nature' of corporate cyberspace.[8]

But the word 'diversity' is no longer spoken only by radical counterculturists. It is the watchword of Britain's New Labour Culture Secretary Chris Smith, and towards the end of her tenure, it was never far from the lips of Smith's Tory predecessor, Virginia Bottomley. Not only has 'diversity' become part of the language of government; it is also a keyword in the new business glossary. While radicals talk about diversity as a bulwark against monolithic corporate culture, corporations such as Rupert Murdoch's News International have embraced it as part of their commercial strategy, especially in relation to satellite TV and their attempts to penetrate Asian markets. Ever since Sony coined the term 'glocalisation' (global organization in the process of being locally adapted) in the eighties, world-class companies have tried to re-orient themselves to take account of local variations in market conditions. This would suggest that the contradiction between corporate culture and cultural diversity has been exaggerated. By the same token, the relatively successful re-orientation of corporate culture during the last ten years tends to contradict the notion of diversity as something which is essentially subversive.

The notion of cyberdemocracy and the idea of digital diversity both contain internal contradictions. Moreover, they are often bracketed together as complementary trends in the development of a new civil society, in cyberspace and beyond. There is a suggestion that the de-centred discourse appropriate to the Internet will lead to the creation of a more democratic form of social dialogue. But this is to lose sight of the really essential aspects in which diversity and democracy are contradictory. Indeed, they might even be said to be mutually exclusive.

The essential separation of diversity from democracy lies in the former's hostility to the universalism which is the *sine qua non* of the latter. Diversity, or the politics of difference, has come to prominence alongside postmodernism as an antidote to the exhaustion of traditional worldviews or 'grand narratives'. Thus Kobena Mercer, one of the commentators who was invited to participate in the Forty Acres and a Microchip conference, has argued elsewhere that 'everybody intuitively knows that everyday life is so complex that no singular belief system or Big Story can hope to explain it all'.[9]

Moreover, in the postmodern discourse of cultural diversity, attempts to explain society as a totality are often identified with repression and 'totalitarianism' – in other words, with the violent suppression of difference. Kenan Malik summed up this illegitimate correlation in his observation that 'not just for postmodernists, but for many postwar social theorists, the road that began with Enlightenment rationalism ends in Nazi deathcamps'.[10]

But democracy stripped of its roots in the Enlightenment is not democracy at all. Thomas Paine, for example, was a man of the Enlightenment who celebrated the historical opportunity to incorporate the universe of experience into a single body of knowledge – what would, in the current discourse of diversity, be dismissed as an illegitimate 'grand narrative'. Paine strove to be a 'universal citizen', and he saw the public sphere as the single, all-embracing space in which human society could address itself as a whole. Thus the universality of Paine's democracy was inseparable from the universalism of his Enlightenment thinking; and it is hard to see how 'democracy' can mean anything much if this essential connection is severed in the name of diversity.

Under the terms of the politics of difference, cyberspace is certainly not the latest manifestation of the single, universal arena which Paine envisaged; rather it is divided up into myriad places, where differences can be expressed and where, by their very expression, identities are demarginalized and authenticated. In this vision of cyberspace, the universe of humanity exists only as a composite of fragments; and in this respect, the contemporary ethos of diversity bears closer resemblance to the racial thinkers of the anti-Enlightenment than to the likes of Paine and his fellow democrats.

It was the reactionary French historian Hippolyte Taine who scolded the Enlightenment philosophers for worshipping the myth of abstract, universal man, and failing to pay attention to the essential differences between real men: 'They did not know that the moral constitution of a people or an age is as particular or as distinct as the physical structure of a family of plants or an order of animals.'[11] Or, translated into current parlance, *vive le défférence*!

Difference was talked up by the likes of Taine and Joseph de Maistre in order to demonstrate the impossibility of humanity coming together for the purposes of democratic debate and decision-making. There could be no coming together, the reactionaries maintained, because there was no common ground on which all of humanity could stand. But at least they recognized that democracy and universalism are inseparable; unlike the postmodernists in cyberspace, who are prepared to deny our common humanity while simultaneously conjuring up a non-existent common cause between democracy and diversity.

One possible explanation for the coexistence of these mutually exclusive elements is that one or the other of them (or both) has been redefined to the point where its original meaning is now lost. The current debate about free speech on the Internet suggests that 'democracy' may have strayed a long way from its original meaning – a society that is controlled by the power (Greek: *kratos*) of the people (Greek: *demos*).

In the mouths of cybercitizens, 'free speech' connotes the idea that all human life should be represented on the Internet, so that when Internet surfers go out onto the Web in search of their identity, the widest range of information and experience will be available to them. In this instance, therefore, 'free speech' means the opportunity to consume online information (which, in order for it to be consumed, must previously have been spoken somewhere on the Internet) for the purposes of self-expression and personal development.

In the period of revolutionary upheaval two hundred years ago, when Thomas Paine's *Rights of Man* was the scourge of anti-democratic regimes throughout Europe, the demand for 'free speech' carried an entirely different set of expectations, none of which had anything to do with self-expression, personal development or cultural diversity. Instead, the champions of free speech saw themselves as contestants in a battle of ideas which would move humanity closer to absolute truth, and facilitate the development of a worldwide society based on universal standards, with each and every individual taking an equal part in the same totality. The aspirations attached to 'free speech', and the expectations of humanity associated with the demand, were of a much higher order than they are today.

Perhaps the most surprising aspect of 'free speech' in its current usage is that it is fast becoming a codeword for the enforcement of today's low expectations. Under the terms of the new definition of 'free speech', the component parts of the old definition, such as contestation in pursuit of absolute truth and universal standards, are taboo. Laying claim to absolute truth is generally construed as an affront to other people's freedom to construct contingent identities based on their own provisional 'truths'. Within the terms of the new etiquette, which is evident throughout society but expressed in a heightened form online, declaring that 'I am right and you are wrong' is considered the height of rudeness. The polite form of expression is to say 'this is right for me (but it could be wrong for you)'. In respectable circles, disagreements are barely tolerated unless there is an element of irony in the way they are posed. In other words, being given a place on the spectrum of diversity is conditional on the place-holder's willingness to abandon contestation as a *modus vivendi* and accept that difference is a virtue beyond question.

Likewise, the term 'democracy' connoted much more in Paine's day than it does now. In cyberculture, 'democracy' is used almost as a synonym for diversity. It implies a social order that is flexible enough to allow many different identities to exist in parallel. But the idea that these lines should meet rather than remain in parallel – in other words, that the minds of all the people should be concentrated on a particular problem in order that they might come to a common decision and exercise their collective power in implementing that decision – is entirely antithetical to cyberculture, and to the contemporary redefinition of 'democracy'. The free contest for power which was always the hallmark of democratic debate has been subsumed into an endless quest for self-expression; and the voice of the majority can be dismissed as 'the mob's baying howl'. Such is the contradictory character of cyberculture that anything approaching democracy would itself be regarded as anti-democratic.

Equality/elitism

In some quarters the information superhighway is billed as the direct route to equality. But others regard it as the terrain upon which a new elitism is already emerging.

The linking of the world's people to a vast exchange of information and ideas is a dream that technology is set to deliver. It will bring economic progress, strong democracies, better environmental management, improved healthcare and a greater sense of shared stewardship of our small planet.[1]

This is how US Vice-President Al Gore described his vision of a Global Information Infrastructure which would have the effect of bringing the whole world into closer connection, and delivering greater equity between the peoples of the Earth. Gore's egalitarian ambitions are widely shared. Leaders of some Third World countries, for example, look to the Information Age as a way of levelling the economic playing-field with the heavily industrialized West. For example, Felix Houphouet-Boigny, longstanding leader of Ivory Coast in West Africa stated that 'Thanks to informatics ... technological shortcuts to development exist today and are within the reach of everyone. We are not therefore doomed to remain undeveloped forever.'[2]

Microsoft CEO Bill Gates sees the information superhighway facilitating 'friction-free capitalism' in which consumer choice is fully extended. But Gates also recognises that RL inequalities will have an impact on life in frictionless cyberspace. 'We are all created equal in the virtual world', he writes in his book *The Road Ahead*, but 'virtual equity is far easier to achieve than real-world equity'.[3]

Many commentators go further, pointing out that far from acting as an equalizer, the route taken by the information superhighway will exacerbate already existing inequalities. In the *Financial Times* survey of International Communications published a month after Gore's ambitious declaration, Andrew Adonis urged 'serious observers to cut through the

35

hype and take a sober look at reality. The fact is that technology is *not* about to "deliver" the GII (global information i-way), and with it a paradise of universal democracy, peace, greenery and long life.'[4] Likewise, writing in the *Times Literary Supplement*, Victor Keegan observed that 'Most of the world's population has never made a telephone call, for the simple reason that the vast majority doesn't have a telephone.' The development of telecommunications is proceeding 'strictly by the market mechanism', Keegan noted: 'the rich come first'. Out of this process a new elite is emerging, the richest of whom (Bill Gates) 'may be able to buy most of the rest of Africa' before his career is over.[5]

Far from being embarrassed about the empire builders in cyberspace, magazines such as *Time*[6] and *Vanity Fair* have run special supplements in celebration of the new information elite. In October 1995, *Vanity Fair* published thumbnail sketches of the top 50 players in what it dubbed 'the new establishment' of the Information Age – with Microsoft's Bill Gates a suprising second to News Corporation's Rupert Murdoch. In third place was Disney CEO Michael Eisner, who is reported to have told friends 'it doesn't matter whether it comes in by cable, tele-phone lines, computer, or satellite – everyone's still going to have to deal with Disney'.[7] Fourth place was occupied by Sum-ner Redstone, chairman of Viacom Inc, whose description in the *Vanity Fair* listing made him sound like an old-school capitalist who just happened to have made his $4 billion perso-nal fortune from entertainment and digital communications.

While *Vanity Fair* luxuriates in the success of the informa-tion elite, critics like Arthur Kroker, professor of political science at Concordia University, Montreal, rail against the advent of a 'virtual class' which 'has driven to global power along the digital superhighway'. The Internet, Kroker warns, has already been subordinated

> to the predatory business interests of a virtual class, which might pay lip-service to the growth of electronic commun-ities on a global basis, but which is devoted in actuality to shutting down the anarchy of the Net in favour of virtual-ized (commercial) exchange.[8]

Along similar lines, many cybercitizens are concerned that the population of the world is set to be redivided into the information-rich and the information-poor. In a world where participation is dependent upon access to information, it is feared that the 'information-poor' will simply not exist in the same social realm as the 'information-rich'.

The contradiction between equality and elitism in the culture surrounding digital communications is succinctly expressed in the debate about computers in education. On the one hand, Al Gore's vague promise of a laptop for every high school student in the USA, and Tony Blair's talks first with BT and latterly with Microsoft about wiring up schools throughout Britain, are redolent with the suggestion that the deployment of digital technology would work against elitism and for egalitarianism in education, and afterwards in society as a whole. In practice, however, everyone knows that the schools with the richest parents would somehow end up with the best computer facilities, thus further enhancing the advantages of their offspring over the rest of the field.

Moreover, in both Britain and the USA, it transpires that electronic education is primarily intended to improve the nation's position in competitive world markets by dint of raising the level of computer literacy among the domestic labour force. Even if at the domestic level there is a genuinely egalitarian intent behind plans to connect schools to the information superhighway, at the level of international relations the prospect of winners and losers is apparently unavoidable, with cyberspace as the new terrain for elite nations to establish themselves at the top of the global pecking order.

So how is it that the technology of digital communications can be invested with such contradictory expectations? Not for the first time, various commentators are vainly hoping that essentially neutral technology will have a necessarily progressive effect on society. This misconception has been clearly exposed by the American critic Langdon Winner in his essay 'Mythinformation':

> Of all the computer enthusiasts' political ideas, there is none more poignant than the faith that the computer is destined to become a potent equaliser in modern society...
> Notions of this kind echo the beliefs of eighteenth-century revolutionaries that placing firearms in the hands

of the people was crucial to overthrowing entrenched authority. In the American Revolution, French Revolution, Paris Commune and Russian Revolution the role of 'the people armed' was central to the revolutionary program. As the military defeat of the Paris Commune made clear, however, the fact that the popular forces have guns may not be decisive. In a contest of force against force, the larger, more sophisticated, more ruthless, better equipped competitor often has the upper hand. Hence the availability of low-cost computing power may move the base-line that defines electronic dimensions of social influence, but it does not alter the relative balance of power. Using a personal computer makes one no more powerful *vis à vis*, say, the National Security Agency than flying a hang glider establishes a person as a match for the US Air Force.[9]

There is little to add to Winner's explanation of the methodological mistake whereby lifeless technology comes to take on a life of its own. But his explanation does not account for the current propensity for making such mistakes. This may have little to do with digital technology itself; indeed it is more likely to be rooted in political and ideological exhaustion, and the corollary of such exhaustion, namely the somewhat desperate hope that technology can function as the *deus ex machina* which will rescue us from the failure of politics and ideas.

Various accounts of the historical examples given by Winner cite the people themselves as the active agents who will bring about equality. In these accounts, firearms appear as merely the instrument of collective action. The people themselves appear to be fired by ideas, and in the struggle to realise these ideas in practice they enter the terrain of contestation – in other words, politics.

According to numerous commentators, therefore, these revolutionary events were characterized by the understanding that equality would be brought about not by firearms per se, but by human beings in their public, political activity. This assumption was itself characteristic of the democratizing dynamic within bourgeois politics, which declared itself with the American Revolution of 1774 and announced its own demise with the crushing of the Paris Commune in 1871.

In the hundred years between these two events, economic activity was also regarded as a route to equality. The eighteenth-century figure of *homo oeconomicus* (economic man) drawn by the classical political economist Adam Smith in his book *The Wealth of Nations*, expressed the idea of self-activating, self-realizing individuals entering on an equal footing into voluntary contractual arrangements with each other. Smith and his contemporaries believed that inequality was an historical remnant left over from the hierarchies of the previous social system, feudalism, which would be superseded as the new society, capitalism, developed to its full potential. Equality, for Smith and other classical political economists, was a function of the new economy in which, besides making money, men also made themselves free of medieval inequality.

In contrast to the eighteenth and nineteenth centuries, the twentieth century has been characterized not so much by belief in political activity, nor by the assumption that economic growth leads organically to an equal society, but by increasing reliance on the state as the sole agent with the capacity to engineer equality.

In the USA, the notion of the state as egalitarian social engineer was represented in grand schemes such as Franklin D. Roosevelt's New Deal and its sixties reincarnation, the Great Society. Similarly, in Britain, the welfare state which began as an instrument for the conduct of the Second World War continued as a mechanism for the construction of an egalitarian-sounding consensus in the postwar period.

More recently, engineering equality across the whole of society has come to be regarded as too ambitious a project even for the state. The spread of positive discrimination programmes in the seventies indicated a diminished definition of equality, which came to mean no more than the (attempted) incorporation of the marginalized into the mainstream. But even this was unsuccessful, and latterly the term 'equality' has almost disappeared from political discourse.

At the end of the nineties, the rival political traditions which formerly offered to bring about an equal society are noticeable by their absence. But our society cannot forget about equality altogether: to do so would be to deny its own foundations. In this context, the responsibility for delivering an equal society is falling increasingly – and impossibly – upon technology.

The earliest indication of the coming shift in responsibility could be heard in Harold Wilson's promise to reforge Britain in 'the white heat of the technological revolution' – a promise made at the last Labour Party conference before Wilson's election victory in 1964, and which, as Paul Foot explained in his book *The Politics of Harold Wilson*,[10] embodied Labour's turn towards technology in retreat from political dilemmas and problems with which it was not ideologically equipped to cope. Three and a half decades later, ideology has been found totally wanting, and technology is even more in demand as the putative equalizer which can reach beyond the diminished range of politics.

However, the forlorn hope that technology might somehow compensate for the failure of political ideology coincides with other ideological currents in which technology is seen as the instrument that has brought about the destruction of nature and the corruption of human society. Moreover, the Green ethos holds that destruction and corruption have come about through the use of technology as the primary instrument in the realization of financial profits enjoyed by the elite. Under the terms of this outlook, therefore, technology is the first weapon of elitism.

The contraflow of these diametrically opposed currents (technology as compensation for political exhaustion/technology perceived as destruction and corruption for the sake of financial gain) provides the context in which digital communications are called upon to deliver equality and at the same time vilified as the sharp-edged tool of the new elite.

Free/fee

Opinion has been divided as to whether cyberspace should be free to all-comers, or whether it should be a marketplace like everywhere else.

'Information wants to be free.'
'Don't copy that floppy.'

These postmodern proverbs encapsulate the division in cyberculture between those who hoped that the Internet would remain outside the market economy, and those who are keen to apply the traditional concepts of ownership and private property to the new marketplace in cyberspace.

The origins of the first strand of opinion are to be found in the counterculture and in the remnants of the Left. Thus the countercultural ethos of communal sharing finds expression in the cybercultural notion of shareware: computer programs which anyone can download for free, provided that they are not then used to make money. Likewise, for many of the hippyish pioneers of the World Wide Web in the late eighties and early nineties, the 'money system' was anathema, and online advertising was tantamount to pollution.

Recognising the influence of the counterculture upon cyberculture, business-oriented futurologists have noted that the cultural baggage carried by many Internet users makes them hostile to commerce and opposed to the use of the Net for sales and marketing purposes.

In *The Independent*, Andrew Orlowski explained how the 'no profits' ethos was factored into the Internet:

> At times it seems like Adam Smith has got lost in cyber-space. Much of the fabric of the Net was created with normal commercial imperatives suspended: from the transparent technical protocols down to the shareware, it is impossible to avoid people who have offered their work for free or next to nothing...Disdaining mundane com-mercial jobs for more creative academic esoterica, these hackers wrote and extended the Unix system, creating,

41

for example, the TCP/IP protocol: the glue of the Internet. This software was never meant to see the light of day as a commercial enterprise – although it was certainly intended to impress other hackers. The programmers thought: why charge money for something that came free? And why hide your handiwork when you can impress your peers with its brilliance?[1]

In its early years, cyberspace also provided a second home to a generation of erstwhile left-wingers who were in retreat from political defeat. Faced by the seemingly unending ascendancy of the right, embodied in the heavyweight quartet of Ronald Reagan and George Bush (USA), Margaret Thatcher (Britain) and Helmut Kohl (Germany), many of those who in the early eighties might have supported the miners against Thatcher took their radical intentions onto the Internet instead.

The shift into cyberculture represented a further scaling down of political expectation. When the politics of Big Ideas was first discredited in the fifties and sixties, some of the best minds of that generation concluded that 'small is beautiful'. They opted to 'think local'; and directed their energies into setting up communes and cooperatives which were small enough for everyone in them to know everyone else. When this too became untenable in RL, they adopted cyberspace as the place where cooperation could continue unaffected by commercial pressures – or so they hoped.

Likewise, when Dr Timothy Leary found fewer takers for psychedelia as a radical religion, he re-invented himself as the high priest of cyberculture and declared that virtual reality was 'Electronic LSD'.

There is a diminishing spiral at work here: the contraction of politics first prompted the hippies to journey into 'inner space' in the sixties; and when the preoccupation with 'inner space' also came under pressure, not least from the New Right of the eighties, they and their successors moved into cyberspace. Here at last, they thought, was a terrain into which corporate money could not enter. But they were wrong.

The Internet first came into existence as part of the defence strategy of the United States of America against nuclear attack by the Soviet Union. Virtual reality developed out of the flight simulation machines which teach pilots how to fly commercial and military aircraft. In short, the counterculture's claims upon cyberspace hardly match up to the contributions made to its development by industry and the military (the people who also invented the first commandment of commercial computing: don't copy that floppy). Moreover, while the counterculturists were desperate to keep cyberspace free from commerce, the men in suits have been equally passionate about commercializing it. Indeed they hope that cyberspace will be the marketplace which can reinvigorate the world economy.

Incorporating different media into a single stream of superhighway traffic is now the main aim of many established news and entertainment corporations. This would allow for the creative reformulation of information and entertainment; and it would also provide an opportunity to sell these commodities to us all over again. Just as the mass production of the automobile acted as the motor for a whole generation of industrialization, so it is hoped that the provision of paid-for multi-media 'infotainment', together with the re-tooling of commerce around the Internet and internal 'intranets', will serve as the dynamic behind the next cycle of 'post-industrialisation'.

In May 1996, *The Economist* published a survey of the software industry which put the case for personal computing and the Internet as the twin turbines in the economic powerhouse of tomorrow:

> Cheap, global data communications will shape the twenty-first century as much as the telephone did the twentith. John Doerr, one of Silicon Valley's leading venture capitalists, has calculated that the introduction of the PC caused the largest creation of wealth in the history of the planet; just Microsoft, Intel and Compaq between them have a market valuation of $130 billion, more than all the film studios in Hollywood, or all of America's television and cable companies. Morgan Stanley's Mary Meeker, one of the computer industry's most respected analysts, reckons that the Internet has the potential to become even bigger.[2]

In 'The Death of Distance', a survey of telecommunications published by *The Economist* in September 1995, Frances Cairncross noted that 'in 1994 the ten largest telecoms giants made bigger profits than the 25 largest commercial banks'. Cairncross also predicted that:

> the death of distance as a determinant of the cost of communications will probably be the single most important economic force shaping society in the first half of the next century... Its effects will be as pervasive as those of the discovery of electricity.[3]

In the race to commercialize cyberspace, the readership of *The Economist* ('suits') has been joined by a cohort of ex-nerds ('suits with ponytails'). Leaving behind the free-speak associated with 'cyberutopians', they are now competing with the majors for pole position in the digitocracy. This is how managing editor John Battelle summarized the commercial ambitions of his own magazine, *Wired* (US edition):

> People are going to have to realise that the Net is another medium, and it has to be sponsored commercially and it has to play by the rules of the marketplace. You're still going to have sponsorship, advertising, the rules of the game, because it's just necessary to make commerce work. I think that a lot of what some of the original Net god-utopians were thinking is that there was just going to be this sort of huge, anarchist, utopian bliss medium, where there are no rules and everything is just sort of open. That's a great thought, but it's not going to work. And when the Time Warners get on the Net in a hard fashion it's going to be the people who first create the commerce and the environment, like *Wired*, that will be the market leaders.[4]

R.U. Sirius, co-editor of the other West Coast cybermagazine, *Mondo 2000*, was more succinct. In his introduction to the book *Mondo 2000: A User's Guide to the New Edge*, Sirius simply declared that 'Commerce is the ocean that information swims in.'[5]

With so much apparently at stake in cyberspace (the future of the world economy, no less), one might have thought that the feud between pro- and anti-marketeers would now be reaching fever pitch. On the contrary, the level of confrontation seems to be subsiding somewhat, and the two 'sides' now appear to be reaching a form of accommodation with each other. How can this be?

The easy answer is that the former free spirits, realising that they cannot hold out against the pressures of the market, have opted to sell their superior knowledge of the Internet to the highest bidders. A simple case of 'If-you-can't-beat-'em-join-'em'. I myself have shared platforms at conferences with half a dozen individuals who used to talk digital anarchy and who now speak enthusiastically about the commercial potential of cyberspace. But it is not sufficient merely to accuse them and others like them of 'selling out' the ideals to which they previously adhered.

The erstwhile utopians turned pragmatic businessmen have made this personal transition in the context of a much broader shift in ideology. The notion of cyberspace as a place free from the market economy first evolved more than a decade ago. At that time, in the world of politics the idea of an alternative to the market system was not quite dead. Although the leftist route into cyberspace represented in part the rout of anti-market ideas in the political realm, nevertheless the idea that society could be organized around priorities other than those of the market was still current.

Nowadays, however, this idea has lost its currency altogether. The phrase coined by the combative Margaret Thatcher in the eighties – 'there is no alternative' (TINA) – is now uncontested in the nineties. In today's context, the notion of 'free' cyberspace sounds as laughable as the hilarious episode of the squatters in the fashionable West London district of Notting Hill who in the seventies went to the United Nations and asked to be recognised as an entity separate from Britain. At the end of the twentieth century, opposition to TINA seems absurd.

But if the anti-marketeers have conceded defeat – to the point where many of them no longer have a clear idea of what the contest was about in the first place, this does not mean that the pro-marketeers are necessarily triumphant. While there is no plausible alternative to the idea that there is no alternative, not everyone is in love with TINA – not even those whose origins lie in the pro-market camp.

During the Cold War, the claim was frequently made that only the Stalinist bureaucracy and its communist ideology stood between the impoverished peoples of the Soviet Union and Eastern Europe, and the standard of living enjoyed in the market economies of the West. But since the fall of the Berlin Wall in 1989, prosperity has failed to materialize in the East, and in the West there has been nothing – not even the negative advertising formerly provided by the example of the Soviet Union – to prop up the ideological edifice which maintained that capitalism is the best of all possible worlds.

The story of the nineties has not been one of capitalist triumphalism; rather this decade has been one long saga of loss of nerve. Aggressive new rightists have been racked by doubt concerning their own social system. John Gray, now professor of European thought at the London School of Economics, is a case in point. A leading light on the New Right in the eighties, in the nineties Gray has pronounced conservatism 'dead' and accused pro-marketeers of failing to live up to their social responsibilities.[6] He now writes articles for *The Guardian*, a newspaper with origins on the left-of-centre.

Nor is this trajectory confined to academics and ideologues. The senior manager of the nineties, instead of wearing red braces and shouting that 'greed is good', is more likely to be attending a conference on Corporate Citizenship and discussing 'how businesses should conduct their relations with customers, suppliers and the communities they live and work in'.[7]

A similar ethos applies among those at the forefront of commercializing cyberspace. No one wants the reputation of being a fully-fledged champion of the free market; and any attempt to dominate the market is frowned upon, at the ideological level at least. It is far preferable to be known as a facilitator of 'sustainable communities', bearing in mind that corporations are communities, too – and of course they need profits to sustain themselves.

On the Internet, even Microsoft maintains a section of its Network (MSN) which is free-to-view, as well as the pay-to-view 'fee' section which is avilable only to subscribers. This is not because money-grubbing Microsoft has committed an aberration; nor is the 'free' section merely an enticement to join the fee-paying subscribers, although this is no doubt a consideration in the MSN business plan. The broader point is that even the most profitable companies in cyberspace, Microsoft included, require an image of themselves as not just a money-making machine. They cannot look themselves in the eye otherwise.

Instead of a battle between 'suits' and utopians, corporations and counterculturists are remodelling themselves in accordance with the convergence between ideas about society and notions of the market. In a new ideological climate in which the market is seen as both inevitable and irresponsible, they are learning to live together under the umbrella of the 'social market'. Indeed, the corporate 'suit' and the pony-tailed counterculturist are increasingly indistinguishable, as the editor of *Mondo 2000* indicated when he described his magazine's readership in the following terms:

> People in their thirties, people in the computer industry. A large portion of the readership is successful business people in the computer industry, and in industry in general, because industry in the United States is high-tech.[8]

Gates/anti-Gates

Microsoft co-founder Bill Gates is revered as a visionary and reviled as a control-freak.

Q: So in five to 10 years, what kind of company will Microsoft be?
A: We're in four businesses now, and in 10 years from now, we'll be in the same four businesses.

First is the PC operating system. In 10 years, a lot of that will be speech recognition, speech synthesis and vision. It's our second-biggest business and probably still will be.

Our biggest business is productivity tools: Microsoft Office, Word, Excel. Those will also adapt to the world of information on-line. Either that or the operating system will be our biggest.

The third business is our fastest-growing, and that's server software. That's a lot of different products to get people e-mail and databases, all built on top of Windows NT and going under the BackOffice acronym.

The fourth area is interactive content. We've got the Microsoft Network, MSNBC, Slate, Cityscape. We're trying a variety of things. Some won't be successful and some will. Even five years out, they won't be as large as the other three.

Extract from 'What will Microsoft be like in 10 Years?', a Q&A session with Bill Gates, *USA Today* 15 October 1996.

Last year a rebel band of some of the world's biggest computer firms began to argue that 'Network computers' – stripped down computers connected to a network that holds most of their software and data – would shortly overtake the ubiquitous personal computer. The network computer's fan club is led by Larry Ellison of Oracle, Sun Microsystem's Scott McNealy, and IBM's Lou Gerstener. As it happens, these are the bosses of three of the strongest computer companies outside the oligopoly of Microsoft and Intel, which dominates the PC market. They see network computers primarily as a way to break the grip of the

PC, just as the PC once broke that of the mainframe, and hope to make fortunes selling software (Oracle's), servers (Sun's) and mainframes (IBM's) to go with this novelty. Predictably, some of the noisiest scepticism has come from Microsoft, the company that would lose most if the PC went out of fashion.

Extract from 'Weighing the Case for the Network Computer', *The Economist*, 18 January 1997.

This was not a Microsoft friendly conference [Gartner Group conference], and that reflects a wider fear and loathing of the software giant. Netscape CEO Jim Barksdale, who is warring with Microsoft over control of the Internet browser market, launched a number of barbs at [Bill] Gates. At one point he said it was his priority to push for open systems on the Internet so that one platform – ie, Microsoft's – wouldn't dominate.

Extract from 'Coming Down Hard on the Firm', *USA Today*, 15 October 1996.

Bill Gates, like Rupert Murdoch before him, is the man they love to hate. The co-founder and CEO of Microsoft, who has amassed a fortune in excess of $24 billion in the 22 years since he dropped out of Harvard, already had a reputation for sharp business practice (critics accused him of pinching Apple's user interface for Windows 95, for example) before he started looking hungrily at the Internet in the mid-nineties. Now, having recast Microsoft to take account of the World Wide Web, Gates is reviled for robbing the Internet of its countercultural ethos, and turning it into just another marketplace. In his mid-forties, he is still thin and gawky; but to many Netizens, Gates is the ultimate 'fat cat'.

He has his fans, too. Many Microsoft employees agree with Steve Ballmer, one of Gates' key lieutenants and closest associates, that 'he's the smartest guy I've ever met'. There is a saying at the company that 'talking to most people is like sipping from a fountain, but with Gates it's like drinking from a fire hose'.

In *Newsweek*, Steven Levy announced the coming of 'the Microsoft century'.[1] In *Time* magazine, Walter Isaacson described Gates as 'one of the most important minds and personalities of our era', and characterized him as both 'the

Edison and Ford of our age'.[2] But why does 'our age' –
unlike previous ages – have so much trouble coming to
terms with one of its key figures? Does the answer lie in
Gates' personality, or in the character of our times?

Microsoft's opponents depict Gates as at once voracious
(his company is also known as 'Microshaft'), totalitarian and
nerdish. Gary Reback, the anti-trust lawyer representing
Netscape, whose Internet browser (Navigator) is in competition with Microsoft's Internet Explorer, insists that Gates and
his troops 'are trying to use an existing monopoly to retard
introduction of new technology'.[3] Netscape CEO Jim Barksdale believes that stopping Microsoft is synonymous with
preserving freedom of choice. Barksdale explained to *Newsweek*'s Steven Levy that 'the person who spends serious
money for software wants choices and realizes it's in his
advantage to spread the money around'.[4] For Sun Microsystems, Scott McNealy was melodramatic: 'There's two camps,
those in Redmond [Microsoft], who live on the Death Star,
and the rest of us, the rebel forces.' Oracle's Larry Ellison
simply said: 'Everybody hates Microsoft.' On 28 October
1996, Netscape, Sun Microsystems and Oracle decided they
hated Microsoft enough to sign a strategic agreement to
exclusively market each others' products. Known as 'Vendors
Against Microsoft', their coalition was set up with the
expressed aim of freezing Gates out of the market.

Under the banner headline, 'Today the Internet – Tomorrow the World', an article in *The Guardian*'s Online supplement compared greedy Gates to Chairman Mao.[5] The notion
of Gates as some kind of dictator has been endorsed by
former Microsoft employees who, noting the high level of
surveillance on the corporation's Seattle campus, give the
impression that it is almost a prison camp. Gates himself
compounded this negative, authoritarian image when, in
his book *The Road Ahead*, he predicted – without any apparent concern – that 'we could reach the point where cameras
observe most of what goes on in public'.[6]

Descriptions of Gates as a social inadequate are commonplace. In March 1997, *The Observer* newspaper carried an
extract from John Seabrook's book *Deeper: A Two-Year Odyssey
in Cyberspace*,[7] which was not uncomplimentary towards
Gates. Nevertheless, the piece was subtitled 'conversations

with a nerd'.[8] The nerdish Gates 'never really grew up in terms of social responsibility and relationships with other people', according to computer industry guru Esther Dyson. She told *Time* magazine, 'He's brilliant but still child-like. He can be a fun companion, but he can lack human empathy.' *Time* reporter Walter Isaacson, who was largely sympathetic to Gates, could not help comparing him to an automaton when, in answer to a question about the 'special, perhaps even divine' character of the human soul, Gates simply said 'I don't have any evidence on that.'[9]

To his critics, Gates is not only soulless but tasteless as well. Steve Jobs, the co-founder of Apple computers, famously remarked that Microsoft 'has absolutely no taste... and they don't bring much culture to their products'.[10]

On the Internet, anti-Gates postings are as frequent as they are vehement. Cybercitizens welcomed the US Department of Justice's threat to fine Microsoft $1m a day for infringing the rules of commercial competition, applauding it as a brave declaration of war on Gates' megalomania. In 'Gates of Hell', an article in the *Sunday Telegraph* about anti-Gates websites,[11] Matt Labash described how one particular site mixes the idea of Gates-the-nerd with the notion of Gates-the-authoritarian: Gates is depicted as the 'new ruler' of NBC who casts himself in top-rated sitcoms such as *Friends* and *Seinfeld*. 'Bill, you're such a dork', says Rachel from *Friends*; to which the imaginary Gates replies: 'You're fired.' Turning to Jerry Seinfeld, Gates says to him, 'Let's make this show about something.' When Seinfeld replies 'You can't, the show is about nothing,' he too is told: 'You're fired.' This is typical of the light-hearted material to be found in many anti-Gates websites. But some of them are more crude, depicting Gates as Hitler and comparing his book to *Mein Kampf*; and others are coarser still, such as the site which begins 'Bill Gates dies in a car accident...'

The accusation that Gates is a nerd seems particularly ironic. In the *Sunday Telegraph*, Matt Labash noted that the poisonous remarks about Bill's dandruff, his haircut (half-way between a monk and a Monkee) and his erstwhile habit of watching videotaped physics lectures on Saturday nights, are equally applicable to '80 per cent of all Netheads'. This prompted Labash to conclude that 'Gates loathing is a disguised form of self-loathing'. Even if Netheads are not really as nerdish as they are reputed to be, it seems plausible that their dislike of Gates is at least partly fuelled by a desire to distance themselves from their own public image.

The image of Gates-the-authoritarian also says something about those who have formulated it. In many respects, Gates can claim to be as much a part of the counterculture as they can. He did, after all, drop out of Harvard. Like many other drop-outs in the seventies, he set up a business with an 'alternative' flavour. One of his favourite novels is the original tale of teenage angst, J.D. Salinger's *Catcher in the Rye*. In *Time* magazine, Walter Isaacson compared Gates' sense of humour to that of the pranksterish playwright Tom Stoppard. And, like many erstwhile radicals, Gates now sees charity as one of the few remaining ways to make a contribution to society. After another ten years at the helm of Microsoft, he plans to devote the rest of his working life to the project of giving away his rapidly expanding fortune.

But the closest correlation between Gates and the counter-culture is to be found in the working environment which he has established at Microsoft's Seattle campus. After going there to attend the launch of Windows 95, journalist Jim McClellan noted the 'sartorial informality' and apparent 'organisational looseness' on campus. Microsoft staff, McClellan wrote, 'work hard at everything, including having fun and being unconventional'.[12] The atmosphere described by McClellan might best be understood as a hybrid of corporate culture and counterculture, in which the prankster mentality asso-ciated with the latter is applied in the interests of the former. McClellan recognised that this ensemble is held together by the guru-like figure of Gates himself, which 'seductively binds them ever tighter to the company' and to ' "the cult of Bill" '. Again, this kind of cultish personal loyalty is entirely in keeping with the counterculture and its relationship to the successive gurus (Allen Ginsberg, Timothy Leary, Mahareshi Mahesh Yogi) who influenced it.

Novelist Douglas Coupland, whose book *Microserfs* is a factoid account of life among Microsoft employees, sees something insidious in the deliberately youthful ethos of the Seattle campus. In *Microserfs*, one of his characters rails against 'high-tech cultures':

Just think about the way hi-tech cultures purposefully pro-tract out the adolescence of their employees well into their late 20s, if not their early 30s... and the way tech firms won't even call work 'the office' but instead the 'campus'. It's sick and it's evil.[13]

In this brief speech, Microsoft stands accused of fostering an atmosphere in which young people are encouraged not to grow up; and of creating an environment in which the dif-ference between work, study and play is obscured. But both these accusations are equally applicable to the counterculture itself, which throughout the half-century of its existence has consistently put childhood on a pedestal and looked down upon adulthood as 'square' and 'uncool'. Likewise, in its rejection of the Protestant work ethic, the counterculture has always sought to turn work into play and so elide the distinction between them. Hence the managers of 'alternat-ive' businesses have often been heard to say that their staff do not need holidays because they are so 'into' what they are doing.

On all counts it seems that the Seattle campus is the partial realization of countercultural values rather than their nega-tion. Again, it seems plausible that the hostility towards Microsoft and its corporate culture is a form of self-loathing on the part of those who are connected to the counterculture and yet uncomfortable about where it has ended up.

But what of the accusation that Gates is a shark in business, whose gobbling up of competitors is unethical and unaccept-able? Isaacson reports that Gates once e-mailed him a two-page justification of Microsoft's commercial tactics. Gates claimed that:

If improving a product based on customer input is willful maintenance of trying to stay in business and not have Netscape turn their browser into the most popular operat-ing system, then I think that is what we are supposed to do.[14]

Gates clearly believes he is playing by the standard rules of capitalist competition. Indeed, in previous epochs playing to win brought accolades rather than accusations; but the rules have been modified in line with today's climate of apprehension. This is the epoch in which winning has come to be regarded as unethical; and Gates is bearing the brunt of a sanctimonious sea-change in the attitudes of the business world towards itself.

Nowadays capitalism wants to see itself as a 'sustainable society' which recognizes that there are inherent limits (in production, scientific exploration, social experimentation and so on) beyond which we simply must not go. There is no longer a sense of continuous expansion, and the theories of the fifties and sixties which apologized for the status quo by promising unlimited growth, are noticeable by their absence in the nervous nineties.

Today there are continual warnings against economic acceleration, which is often seen as the inevitable precursor to recession. Instead, we are advised that the system works best when it remains within proper limits. Failure to observe such limits is, as Edward Tenner puts it in the title of his eponymous book, the reason 'why things bite back'.[15] In short, the currently fashionable theories of risk society express both recognition of the power of capital and unprecedented fear of what will happen if it is unleashed.

The same ambiguity is made manifest in the contradictory attitudes towards Microsoft and its CEO, Bill Gates. On the one hand, the ongoing expansion of Microsoft is viewed with awe and admiration. On the other hand, Microsoft's unending growth is tantamount to blasphemy in a society where ethical behaviour now means the strict observance of limits. Microsoft is the capitalist success story of the late twentieth century, and negative attitudes towards it are the clearest expression of a social system which has lost confidence in itself, to the point where it is frightened of success as well as failure.

Oddly enough, the same sort of self-deprecation and self-doubt is discernible in Bill Gates himself. Gates, perhaps the most powerful businessman in the world, once explained to author John Seabrook that power is corrupting. 'Being in the spotlight is a corrupting thing', Gates admitted. 'Being successful is a corrupting thing. Having lots of money is a corrupting thing. These are very dangerous things, to be guarded against carefully. And I think that's very, very hard to do.'[16] This sounds like corporate culture in denial of itself.

Furthermore, after their face-to-face meeting, Gates sent an e-mail to Seabrook in which he criticized the arch-capitalist Henry Ford:

> Ford is not that admirable – he did great things but was very, very narrow-minded and willing to use brute force power too much. His relationship with his family is tragic. His model of the world was plain wrong in a lot of ways. He decided he knew everything he needed to know fairly early in his life...[17]

It seems as if Bill Gates, the-man-of-his-times, is so imbued with today's ethical concerns that he might almost lead a campaign against Bill Gates, the-richest-man-in-America. Such is the bout of self-doubt which currently afflicts our society.

Hackers/slackers

The image of dangerous and highly motivated hackers
does not appear to tally with the notion of Generation X
as a cohort of deactivated slackers.

On Thursday 17 November, the Online section of *The Guardian* newspaper carried an article by Nick Rosen about the making of *Hackers*, a film by Ian Softley whose first movie was the Beatles biopic *Backbeat*. Softley seemed to locate hacking in the countercultural tradition of subversive activity when he characterized it as 'breaking society's rules as an expression of freedom and character'.[1]

Exactly one week later, on Thursday 24 November 1994, *The Independent* devoted its first three pages to the story of how a hacker penetrated the heart of British intelligence.[2] In an article on page three sub-titled 'The Threat', the paper warned that even the prime minister is 'at risk of terrorist eavesdroppers'. A few days later, the *New Statesman* noted that New Labour defence spokesman David Clark had been the first politician to take up 'the devastating national security implications of last week's British Telecom (BT) "hack", which led to intelligence service telephone numbers and addresses being disclosed'. In an attack on the 'complacency' of the Ministry of Defence, Clark was reported to have said that 'the lives of our troops could be at risk if MoD information can be accessed by other countries'.[3]

In February 1995, a book entitled *Masters of Deception: The Gang Who Ruled Cyberspace* was published in Britain.[4] Written by *Newsday* journalists Michelle Slatalla and Joshua Quittner, it told the 'astounding story' of the 'havoc' wrought by 'a gang of seriously underprivileged kids from the streets of Harlem, who souped up the most primitive PCs to become simply the best computer hackers in the world'. According to the press release which accompanied the book, the self-proclaimed Masters of Deception had 'engineered the crash of AT&T' and gained 'access to thousands of bank accounts including those of Richard Gere and Julia Roberts'.

Also in February 1995, the *Sunday Times* reported that the FBI was concerned about Russian hackers 'raiding corporate America on behalf of criminal syndicates'.[5] Arnaud de Borchgrave, director of the organized crime project at the Centre for Strategic and International Studies in Washington, was quoted as saying that the anti-crime 'wars of the future will be fought in cyberspace'.

A few days later, at 2 a.m. on 15 February, US federal agents in North Carolina arrested Kevin Mitnick, perhaps the most celebrated hacker in the three decades and more since computer systems were first broken into. While on the run from the authorities, Mitnick had previously been described by John Sweeney of *The Observer* as 'a technological Lucifer, a brilliant computer whizz kid who fell from grace to hack from the dark side', and as 'a superhighwayman... the Ronnie Biggs of cyberspace'.[6]

Whether they are billed as the latest manifestation of the counterculture, or as a subversive subculture, or as a criminal threat to civilization and private property, hackers are often described in near-apocalyptic terms. However, the manner of Mitnick's arrest, with reporter John Markoff on hand to turn it into an exclusive front-page story for the *New York Times*, prompted suggestions that this particular event was primarily a media opportunity, and, more broadly, that reports of the threat to society posed by Mitnick and others have been hyped out of all proportion.

Likewise, the *New Statesman* revealed that the 'hack' story to which *The Independent* devoted three whole pages of one issue, with further extensive coverage in subsequent issues, was in fact 'not a great breach of security for the intelligence establishment'. Peace campaigners at the National Security Agency's Menwith Hill Base had been far more effective, the *New Statesman* claimed.[7]

So, are hackers really hell-bent on harming our society, or is hacking far less harmful than it has been made out to be? In November 1994, Charles Platt went to the Hackers On Planet Earth (HOPE) conference for *Wired* magazine, and found the attendees to be mild-mannered – even gullible:

> The hackers at the HOPE conference... were more trust-worthy and less threatening than any 'normal' crowd of

teenage males whose idea of action on Saturday night would most likely include drinking, driving, hassling women and picking fights in bars. Hackers, in fact, tend to be quiet, shy, and honest. When a total stranger at the conference asked to borrow my new $500 camera, I loaned it to him without a second thought and was only mildly concerned when he disappeared with it for a quarter of an hour. Compare this with a crowd at a baseball game or a rock concert, and you begin to realise that the 'hacker threat' is about as scary as a kid wearing a Halloween mask.[8]

Platt also witnessed the conmen of cyberspace behaving like suckers themselves. With 600 people queuing up to receive conference badges each of which took at least a minute to produce, Platt noted that

a friendly Dutch hacker with long golden hair and a tie-dyed T-shirt devises an impromptu solution. He goes around selling red numbered pieces of paper as temporary badges, takes US$25 per person, and stuffs the cash in a brown paper bag. No one has any problem with this. No one questions the Dutch guy's authority, or doubts that he'll pass the money to the organisers. And so it seems that the 'devious, unprincipled hackers' are showing an amazing degree of naive trust.[9]

After talking to Eric Corley, the organizer of the conference and editor of *2600: The Hacker Quarterly*, Platt concluded that the 2600 hackers' clubs which meet in cities across the USA on the first Friday of the month must be 'like a giant multinode Tupperware party for the naughty boys of cyberspace'.[10]

Another attack on the hacker's credibility as a dangerous subversive was launched by Vivian Sobchack, writing in *futures* journal. In a challenge to the oft-repeated assertion that 'small groups of individual "console cowboys" can wield tremendous power over governments, corporations etc',[11] Sobchack observed that 'what precisely this power is in a constructive sense is never clearly articulated'. He also criticized the 'hacker/cracker/cyberpunk' mentality ('neither progressive nor democratic') for its diminished worldview which 'cannot envision more than "small group" intervention in the public sphere'.[12]

Sobchack concluded that the hacker 'ideolect' is 'grounded in privilege and the status quo – male privilege, white privilege, educational privilege, First World privilege, economic privilege'.[13] Which would explain why, according to Nick Rosen in *The Guardian*, 'there has been no shortage of companies paying to have their products displayed in the film [*Hackers*], from Jolt Cola to Apple Computer'.[14] Far from being a serious threat to corporate culture, Sobchack suggests that the hacker mentality is closely related to it.

Along similar lines, an article in the American style magazine *Details*, also written after author Emily Benedek had attended the Hackers On Planet Earth (HOPE) conference, hinted that hackerdom is something of a training ground for tomorrow's corporate executives.[15] Benedek claimed that 'Bill Gates started out as hacker', adding that 'Steve Jobs and Steve Wozniak reportedly made and sold blue boxes – devices that emit tones of 2600 cycles per second, which allowed users to hack into telephone trunk lines – before they founded Apple.'[16]

In an article based on Access All Areas, the hacking and security conference which is, broadly speaking, the British equivalent of HOPE, Wendy Grossman collated some definitions of hacking which make it sound less like a subversive threat and more like a pathetic obsession. Rob Schifreen, who hacked into Prince Philip's Prestel mailbox in 1984 and thereby prompted the drafting of the Computer Misuse Act, described hacking as 'still that desperate mentality of sitting there and doing it for hours on end'.[17] 'Emmanuel Goldstein', the name of the virtual dictator in George Orwell's *1984* from whom *2600: The Hacker Quarterly* editor Eric Corley takes his pseudonym, summed it up as 'searching out information and wasting a lot of time'.[18]

Grossman's article concluded with a paragraph about a time-wasting hacker called Zap who 'has videotaped the entire conference before going home and logging back on using his sister's university account to wander around the Internet rattling doorknobs'. ' "I'm just collecting information", he says.'[19]

This last description of hacking bears a close resemblance to the slacker mentality as demonstrated in Richard Linklater's eponymous film, in which the various characters hang out and accomplish next to nothing. A similar kind of purposelessness runs through *Generation X*, the debut novel by Douglas Coupland which spawned a thousand headlines about the lost youth of today.[20] Most of the Gen X newspaper stories were as exaggerated as the ones about hackers. But besides media hype, it seems that hackers and slackers may have some other elements in common.

Perhaps the defining characteristic of the slacker mentality is its indefinite character. The slacker has no agenda, no motive, no direction – hence his avoidance of any form of significant activity. On the face of it, the hacker would appear to be the opposite: his (and the hacker is generally male) is a figure which connotes nervous energy and feverish activity. But perhaps the hacker's feverishness is derived from the same directionlessness as the slacker's sluggishness. In both instances, there is no discernible motive force which drives their existence. The activity of the one is as arbitary as the inactivity of the other. In this respect, hacking and slacking are far from contradictory; indeed they may well be interdependent.

The ethos of the characters in Ian Softley's film *Hackers*, to the effect that there is no right and wrong – only fun or boring, would be equally applicable to slackers. Dennis Hayes also noted the similarities between them in a chapter on 'Computer Builders and Hackers' from his book *Behind the Silicon Curtain: The Seductions of Work in a Lonely Era*:

> Are teenage hackers political terrorists? They are typically white, upper-middle-class adolescents who have taken over the home computer (bought, subsidised, or tolerated by parents in the hopes of cultivating computer literacy). Few are politically motivated although many express contempt for 'bureaucracies' that hamper their electronic journeys. Nearly all demand unfettered access to intricate and intriguing computer networks. In this, teenage hackers resemble an alienated shopping culture more than a terrorist network.[21]

Hacking will almost certainly cause occasional problems for society. But these will be as accidental as the activity itself. Far from being part of a conspiracy against the status quo, the life of the hacker is as random as that of the slacker. Indeed, the origins of both are traceable back to one man who is a hero in both subcultures: namely, William S. Burroughs, the author of *The Naked Lunch*, who went on record to say that he only started writing after he shot and killed his wife by accident.[22]

Burroughs-the-accidental-man is surely the inspiration for the hacker, the slacker and the experience of the arbitrary which they both share along with him.

Innovation/stagnation

According to its proponents, the Information Age is so innovative it is like nothing that has ever happened before. So why does much of contemporary society seem depressingly familiar?

It is 2008 and you are going into a meeting with your bosses. They are in San Francisco and Bavaria; you are in your house in the Scottish Highlands. You sit down in your office, put on a pair of dark glasses and a glove – both linked by wire to the computer on your desk. You find yourself in an electronic 'room' with a table and chairs.

You look around to see your American boss – or rather his hologram – sitting next to you. A moment later the German appears, and the meeting starts. Using your glove you can pass electronic documents around the room – a disembodied hand appears in front of you, to mimic your movements. This is a virtual conference: you found them disturbing at first, not least because you could put your arm through your colleagues. Now you are used to them and feel almost as at ease as you would in a physical meeting.[1]

Writing in *The Independent on Sunday* in 1993, David Bowen depicted a very different way of life on the information superhighway and declared 'the future is virtually here'. In the *Telegraph* magazine, John May labelled 'the shape of things to come' as 'the Knowledge Age' and 'communicopia'.[2] May quoted BT's futurologist Professor Peter Cochrane who promised an Information Age of instant gratification: 'You hit the key. You say the word. You get a response.'[3] But May also cited John Seeley Brown, director of the Xerox research centre at Palo Alto, who warned that the ride in store for us might not always be comfortable: 'The knowledge economy is fundamentally different from the industrial economy, and we haven't begun to come to terms with how different these two economies are.'[4]

Predictions of a vastly different future are not confined to the eye-candy of weekend supplements. In a feature article entitled 'Welcome to the revolution', the blue chip American business magazine *Fortune* suggested that growing up around us is an entirely new 'economy whose fundamental sources of wealth are knowledge and communication rather than natural resources and physical labour'.[5] Warming to the revolutionary theme, Charles Handy informed the pinstriped readership of the *Financial Times* that the coming of the knowledge economy means

> we are seeing Karl Marx's great dream come true in a way which he could never have envisaged. In ten years' time, in most successful businesses, the workers will truly 'own the means of production' because these means will be in their own heads and at their fingertips.[6]

Futurologists John Naisbitt and Alvin Toffler have also averred that the Information Age will be empowering for individuals, who will no longer have to trudge to anonymous workplaces like bit-part players in George Orwell's *1984*, but will centre their life and work around 'electronic cottages' which are as personalized as they are high-tech.

'No question about it', insisted Steven Levy in the American magazine *Newsweek*:

> the information revolution is here. All those ones and zeros we been passing around – the fuel that flames the digital fire – have reached critical mass and ignited, big time. There may still be plenty of stragglers who have yet to nuzzle up to computers, but there is no one unaffected by the explosion of computer technology. Everything from media to medicine, from data to dating, has been radically transformed by a tool invented barely 50 years ago. It's the Big Bang of our time – we might even call it the Bit Bang.[7]

Levy went on to claim that this is a revolution which is 'different from all other revolutions'. He endorsed the remark made by leading Republican Newt Gingrich that 'you're talking about transformations on such a scale that everything changes'.[8] But can society cope with such innovation? Levy warned that 'there's a real question as to whether

our current social structures can accommodate such empowerment'.

While Levy is concerned that we may be overwhelmed by
the pace of change, some commentators remain decidedly
underwhelmed by the elusive character of the Information
Age. In particular, they are suspicious about the way it always
seems to promise more than it actually delivers. In an article
('Before We Rush to Declare a New Era') for the 'Liberation
Technology?' issue of the *Demos* quarterly, the (then) senior
consultant in information technology at the Henley Centre
for Forecasting, James Woodhuysen, contrasted the potential
of IT with its realization:

> For 30 years, the technical potential of IT has often, if not
> always, been undeniable. As a result, IT has frequently
> chalked up impressive achievements – from Telstar to the
> VCR. However, while information superhigways will
> undoubtedly have some impact, the realisation of their
> true potential could well be frustrated by wider social and
> economic constraints.[9]

Citing a succession of false dawns since the early sixties
(Global Village, 1962; Knowledge Economy, 1969; Post-
Industrial Society, 1971; Information Economy, 1977; Third
Wave, 1980; Information Society, 1982; The Age of the
Smart Machine, 1989), Woodhuysen was insistent that 'IT
does not herald a new social system'. Refusing to accept
that current developments in IT mark a turning-point in
history, he located them in a continuum which goes back
almost to the industrial revolution:

> In the long view, IT is but a development of inventions first
> prompted by the growth of the world economy in the late
> nineteenth century. Then, in what Harvard's James Beniger
> dubs the Control Revolution, typewriters and telegraphs
> came into their own because of the need to control the
> accelerated flow of goods brought about by steam-powered
> factories and locomotives. IT also grew up as a symptom of
> changes on the demand side. Since modern mass production
> first overtook the Industrial Revolution, firms have needed
> IT to guide them through markets ever more competitive,
> changeable, diverse and distended.[10]

Woodhuysen went on to suggest that real, qualitative change is to be found not so much in IT itself, but in the newly diminished character of social and economic analysis which ascribes an autonomous dynamic to technology, and ignores the social constraints which consistently override technological potential:

> As the telegraph has given way to the tickertape, telex and videoconference, so new critics have discovered that IT, in its different forms, is the key source of modern wealth. With the end of the Cold War and the collapse of orthodox economics, the roles assigned to capital and labour in traditional accounts of economic growth are no more. Instead, the comfortably neutral framework of knowledge, information and IT comes to dominate analysis. That framework has some distinctly irrational components to it. The mystical aura that now surrounds superhighways contradicts the reality of straitened consumer and corporate markets for them.[11]

Woodhuysen's critical tone seems justified. Despite early predictions of Internet growth which gave the impression that online terminals would already be as numerous as blades of grass, in Britain the constituency of Netizens remains so small that the UK edition of cyberculture's flagship magazine, *Wired*, was selling less than 30 000 copies a month before it folded in spring 1997.

Moreover, the current emphasis on the Internet as the cutting edge of cyberculture is partly a reflection of the slow pace in the development of virtual reality. When cyberculture was first spoken of in the early nineties, VR tended to be more of a talking point than the Internet. The ratio has since been reversed, not least because the relative lack of innovation in VR means that it has so far failed to break through into the mainstream marketplace.

At an early cyberculture event in London, the Culture, Technology And Creativity conference which took place at the Institute of Contemporary Arts in April 1991, the Canadian writer Catherine Richards noted that 'the idea of virtuality in computing is not new'. Recalling that 'the computer-generated image-sound environment was first written about

by Ivan Sutherland in 1968', Richards described how attempts
to manufacture such an environment were beset with difficult-
ies: 'There are problems with the development of VR technology. The helmets are still low-tech and cumbersome. Often
they do not work very well. There is a time-lag in the transmis-
sion of images.'[12] In conclusion Richards said:

> the aspect of VR which has grabbed the public imagination
> is the sense in which it is a visual dramatisation of the
> question of human interaction with computers. It is a
> metaphor for the human–machine relationship. At present,
> it is stronger as a metaphor than as technology.

Richards was speaking almost at the beginning of the nineties. At the end of the decade – at a time when, according to
some of the predictions made ten years ago, we should
already be spending much of our lives in VR – there is little
sign of the realization of virtuality on a mass scale. In this
context, VR's efficacy even as a metaphor is somewhat
diluted.

But virtual reality has always been a dilution of the earlier
expectation of artificial intelligence, as was pointed out by
Richard's co-panellist at the ICA, Ben Woolley, author and
erstwhile presenter of *The Late Show* on BBC2. Woolley
explained that 'artificial intelligence has been something of
a failure. Virtual reality is a response to that failure. It sets
out not to generate an artificial self, but to generate an
artificial everything else.'[13]

So, with the lack of development in VR we are witnessing
the failure, up to now, of a response to the failure to develop
AI. No wonder another panellist at the conference, Kevin
Robins from Newcastle University, spoke about the 'stale
imaginations' exhibited in cyberculture.[14]

The failure to develop artificial intelligence is something
which AI enthusiast Simson Garfinkel was forced to concede,
albeit temporarily, when on behalf of *Wired* (UK) he set out to
investigate the non-appearance of HAL, the AI envisaged by
Stanley Kubrick in the film version of Arthur C. Clarke's
2001.

Quoting David Stork of Stanford University to the effect
that 'what we don't have right' about AI includes 'organisa-
tion, software, structure, programming and learning',

Garfinkel admitted that 'it's a dramatic ideological reversal from the 1960s, when AI researchers were sure that solutions to the most vexing problems of the mind were just around the corner'.[15]

Along similar lines, Woodhuysen noted the merely 'modest penetration' of robots into manufacturing, despite repeated declarations to the effect that they were about to transform the production process:

> Right up to the early 1990s, many commentators still felt that factory IT heralded a new era of 'flexible specialisation' in manufacturing. Assisted by robots, even relatively small firms could for the first time profitably exploit low-volume niche markets. Robots, helped by barcode scanners at retail checkouts, would enable firms to respond flexibly to market changes. By churning out only popular lines, or by assembling themselves based on computer-aided designs, robots and all the rest of IT would broadly allow the 'mass production of individualised products'.
>
> In fact the robots are crawling, not coming. By the year 2000, human beings will still outnumber the world's industrial robots by 6000 to 1.[16]

Even in the spheres where it does exist, such as cultural production, new technology may be more gimmicky than genuinely innovative. Althouth he was more impressed with the work of independent multimedia producers The Future Sound of London, in reviewing new products from major companies for the *New Statesman and Society*, Mark Prendergast felt compelled to conclude that they were not particularly innovative, and that 'CD-Rom wasn't built in a day':

> Costing a quarter of a million pounds to produce, [Peter] Gabriel's CD-Rom [*Xplora*] retails at £39.99. It gives an exciting insight into the making of his 1992 album *US*, the working of his Real World studio complex in the west country, the Womad festivals and much else. One can re-mix *Digging the Dirt* and have fun passing through all the worlds and levels that Gabriel has built into the system. Yet, as a myriad of visual, textual and musical information came out of the Apple Mac, I asked myself: 'Is this interaction or

promotion?' For all its brilliance, the consumer is still at the mercy of the given material.[17]

Nor was Prendergast impressed with the interactive CDs (CD-Is) developed and made by the Anglo-Dutch corporation Philips:

Todd Rundgren's *No World Order*, the world's first interactive title from Philips, is a gross disappointment. Images are restricted to a still image of Todd (the early seventies equivalent of Prince and producer of *Bat Out of Hell*) and some swirling snow and rotating colour bars. These can be moved around to the music, but who cares?[18]

Prendergast concluded his article with a quote from the best-selling techno-musician known as the Aphex Twin:

All these interactive games on CD are really poor. They keep using the wrong material and the wrong technology. I think it could be useful in the future, but at the moment there's a lot of talk about something that's not really anything.[19]

Even the 'talk about something that's not really anything' may not be really new. One of the most talked-about aspects of the Internet is its non-linearity. The absence of a centralizing focus means that, as Gertrude Stein once said of surburbanized American cities, 'there's no there there'; neither is there a beginning or an end to the Internet, and there is certainly no direct route across it. The de-centred character of the Internet is said to have prompted a more diffuse way of thinking and doing among its users. But non-linearity is not, in fact, exclusive to the Internet, as Chris Locke, the Xerox lecturer in Electronic Communication and Publishing at University College, London, has pointed out:

To say non-linearity arrives in the nineties is ridiculous. So-called 'new media' is a convergence of existing media and cultural practices. There's a whole host of things we bring with us when we look at a Web site. This type of structure has been around for hundreds of years. Look at *Tristram Shandy*.[20]

It seems, then, that the discontinuities between the present and the past have been exaggerated. In order to assess the extent to what we are living in an Information Age that is categorically different from the society which preceded it, perhaps it would be useful to periodize the application of information technology in commerce and industry.

In the sixties and seventies, mainframe computers were used in the processing of orders and to facilitate the organization of production. Large-scale data-processing became the norm in some parts of the service sector, for example, banking.

In the eighties, PCs were introduced into accounting, and from there they made their way into other service activities. IT was a necessary part of materials resource planning systems modelled on the just-in-time (JIT) principle. IT became central to sales order processing. In many instances computers were used to do the same jobs as typewriters, but to a higher standard.

In the nineties, IT has been an integral component in multi-skilling, with one user doing many tasks at a single computer screen. Workflow systems allow for the computerization of more commercial operations. The use of internal networks facilitates the rapid dispersal of information within companies. In a bid to cut costs, IT has also been used as part of the process of breaking up large companies into smaller profit centres.

According to *Fortune*, the Information Age began in 1991, the year in which US commercial spending on IT exceeded expenditure on standard equipment. In, for example, 1992, $105 billion was spent on standard equipment and $130 billion was invested in IT. As noted in *The Economist*, as a percentage of the total capital employed in services, the amount spent on IT per US service worker doubled between 1980 and 1990 (from 7 per cent to 14 per cent).[21] But the productivity of the service sector failed to rise accordingly. Not until the early nineties, when the recession acted as a shot in the arm of the service sector, did productivity growth reach 3 per cent per annum.

In 1990 an authoritative survey of the European implementation of IT in health, retail and banking concluded that it had not been used to anything like its full potential:

In our case histories opportunities for organisational innovation appear to have been realised very infrequently.

In most instances, the possibility of organisational change was not even discussed before the introduction of new technology, apart from the outstanding exception of Sweden. This omission seems extraordinary when placed against the scale of funding and risk involved in the investment in the new technology.[22]

From this it would seem that in the eighties IT in the form of cheap personal computers was introduced into many workplaces, but without restructuring the nature of the activity undertaken there. Essentially, computers on desks did what typewriters had done before. In the nineties, recessionary pressures forced companies into making more significant changes. IT played an important role in their attempts to cut the workforce while raising productivity. But the productivity gains which have been realised arise mainly from multi-skilling, where one employee works harder and performs additional tasks previously assigned to another worker.

In industry and commerce in the nineties, therefore, IT has been used primarily to intensify work, or as part of corporate restructuring. In the major economies, it has not been used systematically to transform the way in which people work. The paperless office remains a prospect for the future, even though its imminent arrival has been writ large over reams of newspirnt.

Woodhuysen was right to point out that neither IT nor any other technology can be the determining factor in economic growth and social development. At present, as Woodhuysen intimated, far from being the driving force in society, the transformative potential of IT is being driven back by economic and social constraints.

For example, although it is technicallly possible to reorganize the entire world economy around IT, to accomplish this would require the wholesale abandonment of existing set-ups in both manufacturing and services, together with new investment on a truly awesome scale. This sort of concerted effort is highly implausible, given the incoherence of our 'anti-social society' and its dependence upon the organized chaos of market competition.

One side-effect of the latter is the absence of common standards in IT. An immediate practical problem is the clash of formats and regulatory procedures between media companies and telecommunications enterprises. The ongoing argument about the adoption of a universal language for the Internet is another example of the fragmented character of our society and its hostility towards standardization. Yet without common standards, the transformative potential of IT will continue to remain largely untapped.

Some commentators have compared the application of IT to the introduction of electricity into industry. Electricity was not used effectively until 20 years after the first power stations came on stream; and IT, it is argued, requires an even longer learning curve before coming into its own. The comparison is indeed apposite, but not in the way it was intended.

The adoption of electricity in Western factories came about as part of the reorganization of manufacturing prompted by war. Even in the period between the two world wars, there were no standardized currents or voltages in Britain. State regulation began in 1919 in the aftermath of the First World War, but the standardization of electricity supply and its across-the-board implementation in manufacturing were not completed until the Second World War prompted the restructuring and re-equipping of the production process.

By the same token, the fragmented character of everyday commerce is unlikely to provide the basis for standardizing IT; nor will the marketplace come up with the huge investment which would be required for IT to be applied universally. Only in extraordinary circumstances, such as war, is the constraint of profitability lifted temporarily from the sphere of technological development. In the meantime, substantial investments in IT will continue to be made; but investment will also continue to be directed towards the survival of individual companies in an essentially sluggish economy, rather than playing a part in the total overhaul of society and its means of production.

But if the application of technological innovation in society is currently much slower than has been widely reported, what then accounts for the equally widespread suggestion that we are living in an entirely new age?

In every aspect of contemporary life traditional institutions have been found wanting; many are close to collapse, or else they have already been replaced; and there is a general sense of impermanence. In some areas, change is welcomed, as in the popular embrace of Tony Blair's New Labour. But in most spheres of activity, change connotes the loss of valued tradition and highly prized stability. Taken together, the perceptions of change in all aspects of our lives add up to an apprehensive sensibility in which human beings have come to be regarded as merely the passive recipients of random new developments, and change itself is seen as something which takes place in a realm beyond our control.

The already existing sense in which humanity seems to be dwarfed by events and processes beyond our ken gives rise to the predisposition to exaggerate whatever changes do take place, and to imagine larger-scale changes which are not, in reality, occurring.

Neither is the tendency to exaggerate change held in check by any kind of rigorous critique. In previous periods, social developments and our understanding of them were interrogated by competing social classes and their respective intellectuals. In today's context, however, the exhaustion of class conflict means that there is no pressure to interrogate events from a theoretical standpoint, or to formulate an ideologically coherent position upon them. Indeed coherence is derided as 'dogma', and personal opinion is generally considered preferable to objectively verifiable truth. Cyberculture is the arena where such subjectivism is most advanced; and, appropriately enough, the advance of cyberculture, and its supposed qualitative break from the past, are notions which are only rarely approached with any degree of objectivity.

So it is that we live in a society which, for all its feverish activity, remains essentially stagnant. Meanwhile the diminution of its powers of self-understanding and critical analysis has given rise to a grossly exaggerated sense of change and discontinuity. Hence the contradiction between 'innovation' and 'stagnation' in cyberculture and beyond.

Journalism/personalism

Journalism developed along with mass circulation newspapers and *broadcasting*. What will become of it in an era of online *narrowcasting* and personalized news?

'All the news that's fit to print', reads the proud motto of America's most renowned paper, the *New York Times*. Little could Adolph S. Ochs know that when he coined it a hundred years ago that with only slight editing, it could serve as a slogan for the 21st century, too: all the news that fits. The information revolution is giving birth to the ultimate in niche-market publishing: a niche of one. Some call it *The Daily Me* – customized news, filtered by computer to reflect *my* personal interests, and downloaded to me automatically every morning without benefit of either printing press or delivery boy.[1]

Headlined ' "The Daily Me" ', Peter McGrath's column in *Newsweek* magazine described the advent of online services such as the Journalist programs offered by CompuServe and Prodigy, which retrieve relevant items from news databases according to your personal list of preferences. 'Do you like business news but not foreign?', McGrath inquired. 'Showbiz but not sports? Journalist arranges those into The Daily You.'

In December 1994, *The Guardian* issued a mock-up of how a personalized newspaper might appear in ten years' time. The mock-up included a list of the personal news options 'currently selected' by an imaginary reader, 'ageing slacker' Andrew Bodle. The Bodle preferences were as follows:

> Daily reading time: 52 minutes. Preferred reading level: FOG Index 112. Text/picture ratio: 4:1. Prose granularity: high/medium. Facts/comment ratio: 1:2. Serendipity level: 60 per cent. Permitted interruptions: TV scheduling/weird science. Preferred metaphor: pop lyrics of the 80s/90s/00s.[2]

At the News World 95 television conference in Berlin, Tony Hall, managing director of BBC news and current affairs, asked 'is this the start of news for you – no longer broadcast news, but news tailored to the individual, to their needs?'[3]

In the *Financial Times*, Victoria Griffith reported that 'the electronic Daily Me is no longer a pipedream'. Writing at the end of July 1996, Griffith noted that:

> the last few months have provided a glimpse into the future with the launch of three primitive versions by Point-Cast, the *Wall Street Journal* and the Microsoft Network. The services offered by the *Wall Street Journal* and by the Microsoft Network are alike in that both provide a news service filtered according to subjects nominated in advance by subscribers. PointCast, by contrast, allows subscribers to receive a personalised computer news service on their desktop machines via the Net, with various options including general news, sport and business. Subscribers can also select companies they want to hear about.[4]

Of course newspaper readers have always scanned for items of particular interest to them; and the production of news is itself a selective process based on the 'news values' (moral and ideological as well as professional) of individual reporters and editors. Nevertheless, the trend towards the reformulation of news into something like *The Daily Me* represents a qualitative shift in the function of journalism and our relationship to the news. Even the very name of the British *Broadcasting* Corporation may have to be changed as we enter into the era of online narrowcasting.

Griffith recalled that:

> Thirty years ago, most Americans tuned into one of three chief television network broadcasters – ABC, NBC or CBS – for their nightly news. Announcers like John Chancellor and Walter Cronkite were fatherly figures who helped guide viewers through the events of the day. The result was often national consensus.[5]

This last seems something of an exaggeration. Griffith was talking about a period, 'thirty years ago', when American society was deeply divided over its role in the Vietnam War; and Cronkite, for example, was reviled as much as he was revered. However, although there was widespread disagreement about policy, until recently there has been a consensus about what constitutes news. Headline news has been broadly defined as those events which are relevant to large numbers of people in a particular society. But under the terms of *The Daily Me* model, relevance to the mass of the population is no longer an important criterion. Personal preference is the beginning and end of what constitutes 'personalized news'.

Some commentators have criticized narrowcasting in terms of its propensity for narrow-mindedness. Griffith cited Stan LePeak, a Net analyst at the market research company Metagroup, who 'believes *The Daily Me* may further shield the uninformed from reality', in that it encourages viewers to screen out information which does not match their personal preoccupations. LePeak concluded that 'this could exacerbate the dumbing down of America'.[6]

Likewise, in the London *Evening Standard*, Mark Edwards observed that broadcasting and the national press currently fulfil a valuable role which narrowcasting can never play: 'The mass media provides our common ground, our shared experience. It plays a vital part in bonding us together, in giving us a sense of community.'[7]

Edwards predicted that 'MeTV won't work...because MeTV would mean the end of all those conversations beginning "did you see...?".' But the fact that what we saw on television last night is what constitutes much of 'our common ground' today, is itself an expression of the same erosion of public space which is further represented by the trend towards *The Daily Me*.

When newspaper journalism came into its own in the mid-nineteenth century, its function was to equip the reader with information which would allow him to take a full and active part in public and political life. The description of the power of the press written in 1842 by the young Karl Marx, then editor of the soon-to-be-suppressed *Rheinische Zeitung*, points to the truly empowering role of journalism at that time:

What makes the Press into the most powerful lever of culture and the intellectual education of the people is precisely that it transforms material battles into ideal battles, the battle of flesh and blood into that of the spirit and intellect, the battle of necessity, cupidity and empiricism into one of theory, understanding and form.[8]

For Marx, then, journalism was an essential component in transforming sectional self-interest into knowledge that would benefit humanity as a whole. Journalism would contribute to the appropriation of the truth, which thereby became the property of all human beings: 'Truth, furthermore, is common to all – it does not belong to me, it belongs to everybody. It possesses me, I do not possess it.'[9]

The trend towards *The Daily Me*, by contrast, is antithetical to the notion of journalism as facilitating 'truth' which is 'common to all'. It negates the notion of a public realm which 'possesses me'. Instead it confirms the privatized individual as the possessor of information which he finds personally useful. This outlook affects not only the consumption of news, but also its production. In traditional journalism, it has been the role of the editor, as the representative of the public realm, to demand that the writer must check his individual outpourings against agreed standards of objectivity and truthfulness. In cyberculture, however, editors are noticeable by their absence; and agreed standards of objectivity and truthfulness are even more elusive.

The trend towards *The Daily Me* is most clearly expressed in cyberculture, but by no means confined to it. In the sixties, Tom Wolfe invented what became known as 'New Journalism'. Wolfe gave up trying to write about American youth culture in objective terms; instead he emphasized his own personal feelings about his subjects, thereby introducing the journalist-as-character-in-his-own-story. In the late sixties and seventies, the papers and magazines of the counterculture reflected a shrinking agenda and a diminishing range of increasingly personalized concerns. Nowadays new stories are often indistinguishable from op-ed pieces; even broadsheet newspapers treat news as the personal experience of their own reporters; and the world of print is made up of an increasingly large number of specialist publications. The same trends are equally discernible in television, to the point where the company which produced the Queen's Christmas 1997 broadcast advised her to introduce an element of narowcasting by filming a range of local interludes which would be shown only in the relevant countries. As LePeak observed when questioned by Griffith, 'fragmentation has already occurred to a large extent, with specialised publications and cable [TV]'.[10]

Such developments not only reflect the fragmentation of society, they also point to the fracturing of the role of the individual within it. In the 1840s, individuals saw themselves as active agents in history, and the information provided by journalists was an essential weapon in their intellectual armoury. A century and a half later, we tend to see ourselves primarily as consumers. For us, information is for grazing. It is there to be selected and picked at like any other item of consumption in the supermarket of lifestyle.

In the break-up of the public realm and its manifestation in the journalism of the mass media, we are witnessing the breakdown of the concept of the active individual and the advent of a more passive mode of existence in which events in the world tend to appear to us as merely the extension of consumer choice.

Knockers/boosters

The opponents of cyberculture seem to outnumber its champions. New technologies have always attracted criticism. But digital technology is opposed by those who might, in other circumstances, have been expected to champion it.

Since 1975, when he produced a paper on the convergence of communications technologies and coined the term 'multimedia', Nicholas Negroponte has been been among the most vociferous champions of the trends which have now flowered into actually existing cyberculture. From his vantage point at the Massachusetts Institute of Technology's Media Lab, Negroponte has urged on technologists and entrepreneurs alike. He firmly believes that 'intelligent' machines will empower us all, and he argues his case forcefully, not least in a regular column for *Wired* and in his book *Being Digital*.[1]

Negroponte's boosterism faces a dizzying array of opponents, however. A fogeyish Ian Hislop, editor of *Private Eye*, asked himself 'Shall I have another pint or shall I go home and surf the Internet?', and replied: 'Mine's a pint, please.'[2] Janet Street-Porter, the Queen of 'yoof' TV, directed a sharp polemic against the self-indulgence of an infantilized Internet.[3] Toby Young, the former editor of the *Modern Review* who now lives in New York, warned the readers of *Vanity Fair* that the Internet might turn out to be 'the CB radio of the 1990s'.[4] But, then again, an industry which has to some extent lived on hype and 'vapourware' must expect a few barbs from sharp-eyed satirists such as these.

Apart from these fairly predictable (though not necessarily inaccurate) criticisms, cyberculture faces another assault from commentators who, back in the days when people were not ashamed to call themselves 'progressives', might well have opted to bend the stick towards its positive aspects. Theodore Roszak is a case in point. Back in the sixties, Roszak wrote a sympathetic if not uncritical account of the counterculture.[5]

But a quarter of a century later, when he came to do the same for cyberculture,[6] he was far less forgiving and much more hostile – even though the latter is in many ways a continuation of the former.

It took more than a quarter of a century for communism to generate a literature of regret by those who lost their faith and subsequently became converts to anti-communism. But cyberculture has produced this sort of reaction in the space of a few years. Most prominent among the converts against cyberculture is Clifford Stoll, whose *Silicon Snake Oil* is subtitled 'second thoughts on the information highway'. The blurb on the cover described how Stoll switched to the Damascene road instead of continuing along the information superhighway:

> Bestselling author and genuine legend on the Internet, Clifford Stoll rendered electronic networking infinitely promising and exciting in *The Cuckoo's Egg* which related the incredible story of how he uncovered a computer spy ring in 1989. This positive view of the Internet's potential benefits has been shared by the media, computer owners and specialists alike. Now, in this myth-shattering look at 'the promised land', Stoll is the first to expose the darker side of the information superhighway, revealing all its hidden hazards.[7]

It is doubtful whether Stoll was in fact the first to do a U-turn and 'expose the darker side' – and he certainly will not be the last.

One might have expected erstwhile left-wing critics to be concerned about the surveillance capabilities of digital technology, while at the same time emphasizing its positive potential. The Bolsheviks, after all, did not feel the need to take against industrialization because it was the property of the bourgeoisie; rather they sought to carry on with the job that the capitalist class could not finish. But latterday leftists James Brook and Iain A. Boal felt so strongly about the misleading 'rhetoric of liberation attached to the information industry' that they chose to entitle their anthology *Resisting The Virtual Life*;[8] as if virtual reality is what needs to be resisted, rather than the virtual extinction of the politics of opposition.

Apprehension about the effects of technology is also discernible among technologists themselves. Among industrialists and academics, widespread concern about the ethics of computing has led to the establishment of institutions like the Centre for Computing and Social Responsibility at De Montfort University. At such establishments, the arguments of the self-confessed 'neo-Luddite' Kirkpatrick Sale, who made his name by smashing an Apple Mac with a hammer, are likely to be as well received as those of Nicholas Negroponte. In fact, they would probably be regarded as two equally valid types of maverick.

Although the Romantic reaction is almost as old as the Industrial Revolution, until recently the Romantics have been in the minority. Thus the right-wing social historian Gertrude Himmelfarb felt able to describe the showcase of nineteenth-century British industrialism, the Great Exhibition of 1851, as 'a single nation sharing a single ethos and exulting in the monumental product of that ethos'.[9] In cyberculture, by contrast, there is remarkably little exultation – even on the part of those who are producing it. Nor is there 'a single ethos' in today's cyberbabble; at least, not on the face of it. Closer examination, however, reveals a consensus against the untrammelled development of technology – a consensus in support of limitations which includes all but a handful of people who are easily sidelined as eccentrics. How ironic that a culture connected to the notion of infinite (cyber)space should at the same time be attached to the perceived need for limits and restraint.

Logical/mystical

Information technology is dependent on ordered, structured processes, yet the Internet seems to thrive on the chaos of mysticism.

Digital Mantras is the title of a book published in 1994 by Steven R. Holtzman, avant-garde composer and vice president of Optimal Networks in Palo Alto, California.[1] It was billed by its publishers, the MIT Press, as an extraordinary blend of ideas from music, computing, art, technology, philosophy and mysticism. In fact *Digital Mantras* is typical of cyberculture in its eclecticism and in its perverse combination of a tradition based on logic with the Nietszchean yearning to destroy all rational thought.

In Part Two of *Digital Mantras*, Holtzman presents a concise history of the computer, beginning with the idea of the calculus ratiocinator, 'a system that reduces reasoning to a mechanical process', conceived by the Enlightenment philosopher Gottfried Wilhelm Leibniz. Holtzman tells us that Leibniz was 'a pacifist in the wake of the wars that had devastated Europe', who

> believed logic could enable sufficient clarity and precision in discourse so that disputes and disagreements could be peacefully resolved. Leibniz believed that misunderstanding was at the root of disputes and disagreements, even of wars, and that the inadequacy of language was at the root of misunderstandings between people. He concluded that it was necessary to bring the clarity and precision of mathematics to language and discourse. Leibniz also maintained that 'given an unambiguous representation of the structure of the world and the rules of logic, the reasoning process could be executed automatically, whether by pen and paper or *by a machine*'.

In Part Three, having completed his history of computing and summarized the incorporation of computers into the composition of music, Holtzman outlined an aesthetic vision which combines logical aspects derived from Leibniz and

others, and mystical elements taken from Buddhism. Digitization, he claimed, would facilitate the re-integration of mat-
ters technological and spiritual:

> Essentially binary, the digital reflection will be the continua-
> tion of the Pythagorean exploration of numbers. Since the
> times of the Pythagoreans, science and technology and
> matters of the spirit have been perceived to be at odds.
> But as we approach the twenty-first century, we can return
> to an integrated view of art, science and the mystical. We
> will find ourselves returning to the mystical traditions of
> the ancient Greeks and Indians. Using the new tools that
> will arrive, we will search for the perfect mantra. In devel-
> oping new digital aesthetics, we have the opportunity to
> integrate technology, science, and the mystical to reveal
> *Brahman* ... we will search for the fractal that captures the
> essence of *Brahman*. The vibration. The structure. Digital
> mantras.[2]

Here Holtzman renounced the last vestige of rational argument and broke into its antithesis: prayer. 'In studying OM',
he concluded:

> we seek its essential structure. In understanding the
> essence of its vibration, we understand the essence of the
> Vedas. We reveal the utmost power and mystery. We reveal
> the creation of the universe [OM]. This imperishable Syl-
> lable is All. That is to say: All that is Past, Present, and
> Future is OM; and what is beyond threefold Time – that
> too, is OM.[3]

In its recapitulation of the advances made by the human
mind, only to renounce them in favour of an idea of God,
Digital Mantras is a parable of cyberculture.

The cornerstone of cyberculture is the computer program,
which consists of a series of precise instructions to be followed
slavishly by the computer. Everything is ordered: even random numbers on the computer are generated by fixed cal-
culations derived from the time held by its clock.
Computerisation, moreover, involves taking the knowledge
in people's heads and the fixed processes they perform while
at work, and turning them into a set of instructions for a
machine. Cyberculture, insofar as it revolves around com-

puters, is a continuation of the humanist tradition of applying logic in the attempt to gain mastery over the world in which we find ourselves.

Along with the rest of society, however, cyberculturists are generally preoccupied with the limits of logic, and this pre-occupation often involves devotion to eclecticism and the non-rational. In this respect, cyberculture is a form of high-tech superstition; humanism in denial. Many cyberculturists end up subsuming the legacy of logic within the rubric of mysticism. Yet the contradiction between the rational and the religious in cyberculture is itself susceptible to rational analysis.

Rationality is both an instrument in the production of society and a reflection of the extent (limited as yet, but significant none the less) to which we already control our destiny. But the chaos of the market system in which we live is as tangible as its inexorable logic. In this ambiguous con-text, the real limitations to our control over society morph into the fantastic notion of the divine. The notion of the more-than-human is in fact a reversed-out representation of our current failure to realize the human potential.

The history of religion, however, is also the history of humanity gaining more control over the world. Modern religions have tended to reflect this historical development by gradually making humankind into the centrepiece of their own belief systems – until recently. In recent years, there has been a backlash against rationality and the disasters which are erroneously understood to have been caused by it. The result is a new form of religiosity which is singularly lacking in the human spirit.

In cyberculture and elsewhere, the new religiosity does not even believe in itself. According to the commandments of high-tech superstition, it is sinful to think that one's own beliefs might be applicable to anyone else; and to attempt to convert other people is tantamout to blasphemy. This is religion as a uniquely personal mission statement.

It transpires, therefore, that the new mysticism is not wholly communion at all, but a peculiarly alienated form of self-expression; an inverted form of me, myself, I. In this respect, it connects with the tendency in cyberculture to privilege personal expression above any other consideration.

The personalization of religion reflects the fragmentation of society. But the process of fragmentation has also affected the now highly individuated self which the new religiosity seeks to express. Cyberculture is well known for its hostility to narrative progression – hostility which is epitomised in the fashion for hypertext, lateral thinking and non-linearity. Ostensibly the means to escape the mental straitjacket of failed rationality, these pick'n'mix, hop'n'skip trends are really representative of the extent to which a coherent, consistent sense of self is increasingly implausible in today's circumstances. The fragility of the contemporary sense of self can only add to the appeal of mysticism; which in its current, highly personalized form can only confirm the fragility of the self; and so on...

In the high-tech superstition which is to be found in cyberspace, the human spirit has been broken into an infinite number of alienated fragments. Providing an historiological explanation for the incoherent worship of the irrational is one of the first steps towards the restatement of rationality and our common humanity.

M-o-R/counterculture

Will cyberculture look like middle-of-the-road Main Street, or will it be more like the Woodstock festival? Or maybe there is less distance between them nowadays.

Coping in Cyberia means using our currently limited human language, bodies, emotions and social realities to usher in something that's supposed to be free of those limitations. Things like virtual reality, Smart Bars, hypertext, the WELL, role-playing games, DMT, Ecstasy, house, fractals, sampling, anti-Muzak, technoshamanism, ecoterrorism, morphogenesis, video cyborgs, Toon Town, and *Mondo 2000* are what slowly pull our society – even our world – past the event horizon of the great attractor at the end of time.

Douglas Rushkoff, *Cyberia: Life in the Trenches of Hyperspace* (London: HarperCollins, 1994), p. 300.

Futurologists with an interest in retailing are wont to say that the 'killer application' of digital technology will be ... (wait for it) ... shopping. Instead of shoppers traipsing through dreary malls, the 'electronic mall' will come to us in our living rooms. 'Electronic home shopping', says management consultant George Wallace, 'is like a glacier running through the valley of retailing'.[1]

Computer shopping systems are already available in parts of some Western countries. Residents of Chicago and San Francisco, for example, can shop for groceries by computer using a system called Peapod, and Barry Diller's QVC shopping channel is available coast-to-coast. But, as Louise Kehoe explained in the *Financial Times*, such ventures are 'quite primitive in comparison to the "interactive shopping" planned by several US cable television companies. These services will feature full video and sound, and may provide customers with "agents" to help them shop.'[2]

If shopping does become one of the core activities of digital communications, it will mean that cyberculture has entered the mainstream and severed its connections with the counter-

cultural ideology of the sixties, which Mitchell Kapor was
seeking to preserve when he established the Electronic Frontier Foundation. The Internet, virtual reality, interactive TV –
the whole ensemble grouped under the 'i-way' tag – will have
become as mundane and as middle-of-the-road as a trip to the
hypermarket in the family Volvo, or watching a soap opera on
TV. Indeed the Internet now boasts its own soaps. One of the
most talked-about is *The Spot*, which, as Jim McClellan pointed
out in *The Observer*, has been welcomed by some cybercitizens
and viewed with apprehension by others:

> Created by American ad agency Fattal and Collins, *The Spot*
> has, in less than a year, become an online phenomenon,
> picking up awards aplenty, much media attention and,
> crucially, a fairly sizeable audience who seem committed
> enough to check in on a daily basis. Some enthusiasts talk
> about *The Spot* as representing the future of soap – the
> future of the Web, even. Such talk probably worries Net
> purists.[3]

McClellan went on to say that the 'purists' were beginning to
wonder whether the World Wide Web would be a 'brave new
experiment in communication or merely bad TV that comes
over your telephone wires'.[4]

Major corporations around the world are investing billions
of dollars to ensure that cyberculture is blessed with many
more soap sites and shopping channels, and that 'main-
streaming' is the future of cyberspace. Meanwhile forecasters
like the Henley Centre are helping thousands more companies to incorporate digital media into their everyday business
operations. In these circles, the big idea is to arrive at a
cyberculture for the suburbs primarily by pulling away
from its 'purist' connections to the counterculture.

These connections go back a long way. Some of the brightest luminaries in cyberculture were sparked off thirtysomething years ago by the radicalism of the sixties. Their origins
in the counterculture were obvious to Andrew Brown of *The
Independent*, who observed that:

> The WELL was founded in the 1980s by a bunch of profes-
> sional hippies: Stewart Brand, the editor of the *Whole Earth
> Catalog*, and John Perry Barlow, cattle rancher and lyricist

for The Grateful Dead, prominent among them. Musician Brian Eno is there, too, now.[5]

Douglas Rushkoff's *Cyberia: Life in the Trenches of Hyperspace* is, broadly speaking, the New Edge equivalent of *The Electric Kool Aid Acid Test*, Tom Wolfe's account of the psychedelic medicine show which brought acid and the Grateful Dead to the hip kids of California.[6] Rushkoff locates cyberculture in the countercutural tradition of experimentation, personal growth and non-conformity. Though he started out as more of a straight journalist, he has come to resemble his subject-matter; and when I interviewed him for *Living Marxism* magazine in 1994, he struck me as being in the tradition of rebel icons such as Lou Reed, Frank Zappa and *Mad* magazine.

When I met William Gibson shortly afterwards (Gibson wrote the highly influential novel *Neuromancer* and coined the term 'cyberspace' which he defined as 'the place where the bank keeps your money', he seemed even more redolent of the counterculture. Dressed in black leather jacket and drainpipe black jeans, he spoke a little like William Burroughs and looked a lot like Joey Ramone from the archetypal New York punk band The Ramones.

'My native culture is science fiction and rock'n'roll', Gibson informed me. 'Anything else is a thin waxy overlay.' He had been reading Burroughs' collected letters when he arrived in London 'with jet-lag', and was pleased to discover that El Hombre Invisible had once stayed in a house just a few doors down from the hotel in which we conducted our interview. In fact Gibson went on to include Burroughs, Jack Kerouac and James Joyce in his 'native culture':

> I discovered Burroughs and Kerouac at exactly the same time. I came across a paperback collection of Beat writing when I was 12, 13 – I hid it from my mother. At that time I was reading lots of genre SF, and I remember trying to fit Burroughs into that. Around the same time I read my mother's copy of *Ulysses* which she kept hidden away.[7]

His reminiscences about the late sixties indicated that these were his formative years:

In 67, 68 I can remember fairly calmly assuming that the
order of society was going to change so radically in the next
little while that there was no point training for any position
in the world that existed then. I was wrong, of course. In
the States that all got sour and creepy. But going through
that sixties counterculture thing was my formative experience. I was less like a hippy than a proto-slacker. I didn't
like living in communal houses, but I didn't do anything
career-oriented, ever. I sort of backed into being a writer at
the very last moment.[8]

Gibson was in London on a promotional visit. He welcomed the Internet as something akin to the microcosm of
the counterculture which he had written about in his new
novel, *Virtual Light*. Relishing the fact that it 'actually grew'
from the subversion of 'some wacky Cold War scheme', he
spoke enthusiastically of 'the spontaneous generation of the
Internet, this global system that no one really owns and lots
of people use...for free – it's like the Bridge Culture in
Virtual Light'. But he ended on a note of warning: 'I don't
know if it's going to last. In the past few years, we are starting
to see the law coming to the Wyoming of cyberspace. The
wilderness is being colonised.'[9]
Gibson has expressed similar concerns on other occasions.
But how accurate is the picture of a wild counterculture
being tamed by the coming of the law to cyberspace? Given
the increasing propensity for certain individuals to exist
simultaneously in circles associated with corporate culture
and in networks connected to the digital counterculture, it
may be somewhat misleading.
Gibson himself had been conversing with the Clinton
administration. 'Several months ago Bruce Sterling and I
were invited to Washington DC', he reported. The two
cyberpunks went to meet the government, and 'told
them, if you're going to produce a generation of computer
literate Americans you are going to lose control of what they
have access to'. In the early seventies, by contrast, countercultural radicals like Jerry Rubin and Abbie Hoffman would
never have gone there in the first place: at the time, they
would not have been seen dead in the HQ of 'fascist
Amerika'.

Likewise, Douglas Rushkoff has advised companies such as Sony and The Discovery Channel on how to get in touch with Generation X. In *Cyberia*, he notes that even the most far-out cyberculturists are also career-oriented (unlike William Gibson and thousands of his contemporaries):

> The public relations game is played openly and directly in Cyberia. As we've seen, people like Jody Razdik, Earth Girl and Diana see their marketing careers as absolutely compatible with their subversive careers. They are one and the same.[10]

The increasingly close correlation between mainstream marketing and the 'subversive' was reflected in the usage of the term 'Generation X'. Coined (or, rather, recycled: Generation X was the name of a punk band in the seventies, and the title of a journalistic investigation into the youth of the sixties) by Douglas Coupland in his eponymous novel, Generation X was at once shorthand for a cohort of alienated young people and a blank name tag used by business people to identify the youngsters whom they do not know how to reach. Moreover, these two usages were closely related. Indeed only as abstractions can they be separated out. Similarly, in the late nineties it is increasingly difficult to abstract the values of corporate culture from those of the counterculture.

While counterculturists are acting more like business people, corporate executives no longer see themselves as straightforward 'organization men'. Instead they often explain themselves in terms which would not seem totally out of place in the counterculture, as Barry Diller (the former chairman of Fox who left to take over QVC) did when he addressed the Edinburgh Television Festival in 1994:

> From my earliest days at ABC, I was involved in projects and programs that most of the network thought would fail. Maybe that's why they let me do them. They didn't all fail – or else, I suppose, I wouldn't be here. The reason people thought they would fail always was that these ideas simply didn't conform to the conventional wisdom, about what had worked before or what was predictable by the evidence of the day.

> I believe that a capacity for being contrarian and conten-
> tious is a critical part of successful editorship... the willing-
> ness and ability to flout the conventional media wisdom – to
> create new genres and formats, to have the courage to be a
> convergence contrarian – will be even more important in the
> future than they are today. The new world order of conver-
> gence will demand it and those that are willing to play it on its
> own wildly unique terms, fortunes won or lost, will have a
> great and joyous time being present at the creation.[11]

Diller seemed relatively unconcerned that 'fortunes' will be
lost as well as won; surely not the attitude of a traditional
corporate executive. Instead, he prioritized the 'joyous time'
to be had at the 'creation' of the information superhighway.
Where yippie Abbie Hoffman famously proclaimed 'revolution for the hell of it', Diller seems to be advocating *information revolution* for the hell of it. Business, for him, is in tune
with the priorities of the counterculture; getting high (legally,
of course) is more important than making a profit.

Now it is possible that Diller is simply an unrepresentative
maverick, or that his ode to joy is merely rhetorical. But
various underlying developments suggest that there is more
to it than that. As well as the technological convergence of
new media, we may also be witnessing a cultural convergence
between former conformists and erstwhile rebels.

When Diller the capitalist spoke of having a joyous time, he
was party to the redefinition of business not as a productive
process, not even as a money-making process, but as an experience to be consumed. The emphasis on consumption, and the
redefinition of ourselves primarily as consumers rather than
entrepreneurs or workers, is fairly new to corporate culture
but has always been characteristic of the counterculture.

In the ontology of the sixties, experience was reconfigured
as something – either pleasant (the trip) or unpleasant (the
bad trip) – to be absorbed by the individual. Counterculturists described themselves as 'cosmonauts of inner space' and
declared that 'revolution', when it occurred, would happen
'in the head'. Hippies, before they became known as such,
referred to themselves as 'heads' – a self-label which reflected
the top priority given to the essentially passive consumption
of their own perceptions. The 'heads' were among the first to

interpret all the activity of society through the prism of consumption. At the time they were bitterly opposed by corporate America and other champions of the 'can do' society; but in the nineties these same priorities seem to have been embraced by the corporate sector.

Giving pride of place to creativity was also a defining element of the counterculture. In the pecking order of celebrated notions, artistic creativity took over the number one spot from the idea of progress. Alongside the substition of expressivity for purposive activity, the recognition of historical development was replaced by the celebration of the present moment, as observed by drama critic and senior Yale academic Robert Brustein in his trenchant comments about youth 'benighted' by 'the willful refusal of past history and knowledge'.[12]

Nowadays, these priorities are not only in the mainstream of pop culture, as in the title of the 1997 Oasis album *Be Here Now*, which itself echoes a statement by John Lennon to the effect that 'the whole Beatles message was Be Here Now'; they are also to be found in City boardrooms and the groves of academe. Indeed it is hard to imagine either the coming (and going) of postmodernism or the recent emphasis on financial speculation except in the context of such anti-historical thinking.

But perhaps the most remarkable cultural episode of the last 50 years is the strange case of the disappearing outsider. In the late forties and fifties, a highly visible minority of young people identified themselves by the fact that they stood outside mainstream society. Instead of attempting to overcome their alienation, either by integrating themselves within the status quo or by seeking to change society into something less alienating, they celebrated their estrangement and made it the mark of their integrity.

They defined themselves as outsiders, and the clarity of their self-definition depended on the clear-cut character of the opposing models of society from which they sought to extricate themselves. The outsiders of the postwar period knew who they were because they knew what they were against: the solid, high-profile entities of The American Way of Life and Uncle Joe Stalin's Soviet Union.

Neither of these models are extant today, which is partly why the present decade has failed to come up with its own distinctive image of the outsider. The difficulty is that there is hardly anything left to identify oneself against (nothing coherent, at any rate); and this problem is compounded by the fact that, these days, the mainstream is the place where no one wants to be. Even new media executives like Barry Diller think of themselves as 'contrarian' outsiders. In this context, there is no inside to be outside of; and the would-be outsider becomes indistinguishable from the rest of the in-crowd.

If the counterculture located itself by virtue of its alienation from both left and right, it is now a casualty of the end of the left/right divide. Meanwhile the new power generation in Whitehall and the White House has grown up alongside the counterculture and the proliferation of its values throughout society. Thus the success and failure of the counterculture are one and the same.

From house music to the House of Commons, the counterculture is everywhere and nowhere. What was the middle-of-the-road is riddled with the same contradictions: no one expects to exist outside the everyday commercial world; yet within the marketplace everyone is pointing to their estrangement from it. This means that Main Street has lost its place on the cultural map. Without an opposition, it too is unable to find its identifying coordinates.

It seems that cyberculture will be neither middle-of-the-road nor a direct continuation of the counterculture. At the end of the twentieth century, these terms are as inapplicable as the political terminology of 'left' and 'right'.

Nostalgia/futurism

Is cyberculture heading into the future, or walking into the past?

The Electronic Frontier Foundation (EFF) looks back to the frontier spirit of the American West in the nineteenth century. Critics of the EFF's libertarian individualism often refer back even further, to the communal way of life which preceded the Enlightenment. William Gibson, probably the premier novelist in cyberculture, acknowledges that his writing voice sounds a lot like that of the thirties crime writer Dashiell Hammett. But Gibson is as dependent on the sixties and seventies as he is on the thirties. At the heart of the short story 'Skinner's Room' and the novel *Virtual Light*, there are echoes of Kensington market and the Roundhouse in the seventies and numerous references 'to some dreadful sixties mythology I don't even want to think about'.[1]

Gibson once told me that his formative experiences occurred in the sixties:

> I'm in the classic boomer demographic. I'm a sixties guy in some ways, although I didn't start producing anything until the late seventies. A lot of what I do must be tempered by that sixties thing, whatever it was. Everything I draw on in the sense of street realism comes from that period. That's the only time I had any direct interface.[2]

Like Gibson, cyberculture is full of retro references: the future has been seen before. Roger Vadim's film *Barbarella* and the *Star Trek* TV series, both dating from the sixties, are among the most popular visions of the future. One of the most influential stories is Gibson's 'The Gernsback Continuum',[3] featuring a photographer who goes back to the gee-whizz future as envisaged in the thirties, and finds himself in a parallel universe where the front covers of sci-fi publisher Hugo Gernsback's *Amazing Stories* magazine have come to life.

Gibson is wont to say that his fiction is really about the present, not the future. But his pre-eminence in cyberfiction also speaks volumes about the present-day preoccupation with the past. Today's focus on all our yesterdays is unprecedented in its intensity; and sampling previous visions of the future now seems so much more manageable than inventing our own.

The preoccupation with the past is not the same as a straightforward desire to live in a previous historical period. The nostalgia in cyberculture, as in the rest of society, is often a form of longing which reflects the widespread sense that we have lost something we used to have (if only we knew what it was, we would not have lost it). In this context, the hope for the future held by many cyberculturists is that somehow we will be able to restore what has been lost, thereby making ourselves whole again. This might best be described as 'restorationism'; and it is often articulated in notions of reintegrating aspects of the past and the present in such a way as to create a holistic future.

Bringing cyberculture's enthusiasm for technology together with the nonconformist spirituality of the hippies was the *raison d'être* of the zippies (variously defined as 'hippies with a zip' and as 'Zen-inspired professional pagans'), according to their founding father Fraser Clark. In *Wired* magazine, Clark described how the zippies were trying to fuse the technological with the spiritual:

> A zippie is someone who has balanced their hemispheres to achieve a fusion of the technological and the spiritual. The techno-person understands that rationality, organisation, long-term planning, consistency and single-mindedness are necessary to achieve anything solid on the material level. The hippie understands that vision, individuality, spontaneity, flexibility and open-mindedness are crucial to realise anything on the spiritual scale...A zippie feels the terror and promise of the planet's situation and is prepared to use anything short of violence – magic, technology, entrepreneurial skill – to create a new age in as short as time as possible.[4]

Wired reporter Jules Marshall observed that the clientele at Clark's club, Megatripolis, was as eclectic as its format:

> The Thursday I went, I met a female professional gambler who 'cultivates her intuition', a middle-aged lawyer, school kids, exchange students, graphic designers, and squatters.

Part lecture hall, part Indian bazaar, part medieval court-
yard, part pleasure dome, Megatripolis offers early evening
talks by zippie thinkers (they call it 'Parallel University'),
trippy visuals upstairs, and ambient dance or a percussion
jam in the 'Virtualitiroom', where a bunch of Macs run the
latest interactive demo from The Shamen, or grainy gra-
phics off some kid's floppy.[5]

Marshall also observed that Serena Roney-Dougal's *Where
Science and Magic Meet* was top of the zippie reading list; a
couple of years later, he might have included *Angels* by the
French philosopher Michel Serres, another book which aims
to reconnect art with science and spirituality.[6] The zippies'
spiritual mentors, Marshall pointed out, came from both
Eastern and Western sources and included Julian of Nor-
wich, Pierre Teilhard de Chardin, the Mahareshi Mahesh
Yogi and the Hindu deity Shiva.

As it turned out, the zippie idea was something of a flop, and
the term itself is rarely used nowadays. But notions of restoring
ourselves by combining cultures and creating a future way of
life by bringing together the past and the present, are now
commonplace throughout cyberculture and beyond.

The same sort of restorationist impulse informs the activities of the 'modern primitives' in cyberculture. Stelarc, for
example, is a performance artist and 'cyberhuman' who sees
a relationship between the future interconnectedness of man
and machine and the restoration of passion and sensation
into our lived experience. At a website entitled 'Cyberanthropology', Steve Mizrach, aka Seeker 1, identified Stelarc
and other modern primitives with the aim of restoring pre-
modernity into everyday life:

Borrowing from the S&M sexual subculture, the modern
primitives suggest that one of the effects of modernisation
and industrialisation has been psychic numbing. People no
longer know either authentic pleasure or pain, and have
forgotten the curious neurochemical ways in which they
are interwoven ... There is this idea of knowing through
pain which modernity has forgotten.[7]

Mizrach also noted that the 'ModPrims' have attempted to
unite the past with the future, and are trying to combine

magic and science, as exemplified in the hackers who call
themselves 'wizards':

> ModPrims also embrace the rave as a sign of the uniting of
> past and future. The rave is at once 'primitive' with its
> gathering of 'tribes' of young people for the experience
> of Levy-Bruhl 'participation mystique' through kinetics
> and MDMA (Ecstasy), and futuristic (or modern), with its
> use of digitally sampled and remixed music, laser and light
> effects, and multimedia expositions. Ravers at once dress in
> a way that signifies past and future – piercing their ears
> with computer chips, wearing 1970s (or earlier) clothes
> with futuristic hologram jewelry, combining the fashion of
> folk and punk... Besides rave and piercing, ModPrims are
> perhaps best known for their attempts at juxtaposing
> magick and science. Publications like Virus 23 juxtapose
> Crowleyan occultism with chaos theory, Neo-Paganism and
> Wicca with memetic and information theory, and use of
> ancient hallucinogens with the latest findings in neu-
> roscience. Shamanism is shown to have a basis in quantum
> mechanics, and Hermeticism in astrophysical cosmology.[8]

The fashion for juxtaposing various elements within a new
epistemology sounds like a welcome break from the trends
toward niche marketing and narrow specialization. But the
resulting combination is by no means as wide-ranging as it
first appears. With unfailing regularity, the elements that are
picked for this mix turn out to be mere reflections of the
contemporary mindset, in all its narrowness and superficial-
ity. Thus the common elements in shamanism and quantum
mechanics are never really 'shown', presumably because they
do not exist; and the connections between the past and the
future are made only at a metaphorical level – the only level
at which they can be made.

For example, in the days before the Criminal Justice Act
1994, some of those who travelled to illicit raves at various
far-flung sites may have liked to think of themselves as noma-
dic tribes. But these 'tribes' consisted of young working-class
people growing up in a decaying capitalist country; and the
suggestion that they were somehow on the same wavelength
as hunter/gathering tribespeople is utterly spurious except as

a not-very-good metaphor for the sense of rootlessness among the young urban population.

The current reliance on past notions of the future suggests that we are increasingly unable to generate an original vision of tomorrow's world. Moreover, the inability to envisage the transformation of society in the future is mirrored by the inability to recognise and comprehend transformations which have already taken place. Today, nostalgia (if 'nostalgia' is defined, loosely, as the wish to live in the past) is as impossible as futurism, because real knowledge about the past is as scarce as confidence in the future. Whatever it is that we are longing for, it is not in the past at all. As expressed in cyberculture and elsewhere, the desire to reclaim the 'past' and incorporate it into the future is primarily an expression of our feeling of impotence in the face of present-day social problems.

Whether it takes the form of nostalgia, futurism or the attempt to integrate the past into the future, what is really being expressed is the yearning to leave the present behind and enter into the contemporary equivalent of religious rapture. As Mark Dery has pointed out in his book *Escape Velocity*, this 'theology of the ejector seat' is a means of sidestepping the real world in which we live.[9]

Overload/information

While some claim that 'information is power', others have come to the conclusion that too much information is as debilitating as too little.

In his column on the Internet for *The Observer*, John Naughton divided the inhabitants of cyberspace into two types:

> One is the information junkie who exults in the cornucopia of online information... Some people, however, are exactly the opposite. For them, the overweening abundance of the Net is its most terrifying feature.[1]

John Browning, executive editor of *Wired* (UK) until its demise in 1997, is a committed infophile. At a conference on the future of the Internet called by a group called Design Agenda, he defined information as 'that which is useful to me', and rubbished any suggestion that information might sometimes be a hindrance as well as a help.[2]

Where Browning was confident to the point of arrogance, Victor Keegan, former economics editor for *The Observer* and now an assistant editor at *The Guardian*, is apprehensive. He has warned that 'in the brave new age of computers and the Internet we are undergoing a daily bombardment of data far beyond our ability to assimilate'.[3] Keegan illustrated his thesis with reference to the shattered career of one Di Harris:

> She had counted herself fortunate. A 23-year-old graduate in a high profile job with an oil company, she was working long hours analysing a sandstorm of corporate data coming at her from all directions: daily sales figures, profit and loss, and budget analysis – all with different ways of accounting and with managers champing at the bit ...
>
> Then suddenly, she could take it no longer. There were headaches, pains in ther arms and legs, a build-up of depression – all related to work. Her doctor told her she was heading for fatigue syndrome and needed to take time out. Di didn't know it, but she had contracted a newly

98

discovered disease that almost defines the end of the century: information overload.[4]

Without becoming allergic to information in this fashion, some of cyberculture's brightest stars are now wary about exposing themselves to an excess of it. For example, in 1997 the original cyberpunk novelist William Gibson spoke to a journalist from *.net* magazine about e-mail avoidance and rationing his time in front of a terminal:

> One of the reasons I don't personally do e-mail is that I wouldn't want to give up the time I have in which I'm allowed not to be sitting in front of a word processor. Having to spend two more hours a day sitting in front of a computer doesn't appeal to me.[5]

Douglas Rushkoff is another prominent cybercitizen who is concerned about being overloaded with banality. 'I am sick to death of new media', he said in an interview for the 1997 Edinburgh TV Festival magazine, 'I go on to the Internet to do my e-mail and get off it as soon as possible.'[6]

Why is it that former devotees of the Information Age are now putting up defences against its allegedly corrosive effects? Perhaps because infophilia and infophobia are but two interchangeable responses to a process which might best be described as the the breakdown of knowledge into mere information.

What Francis Bacon originally said was: 'knowledge is power'. But in recent years there has been a tendency to misquote Bacon and declare that 'information is power'. The substitution of information for knowledge in the latterday reworking of this aphorism is indicative of a parallel process in society as a whole. Where once we had the means of measuring information for veracity and ordering it according to its significance, now it impinges on our consciousness as an immeasurable stream of largely unconnected fragments. For some this is close to liberation, while others feel imprisoned by the process of relativization at work here.

In *Newsweek*, Peter McGrath went some way towards explaining why knowledge is missing from the Information Age:

[T]he implicit epistemology of the information superhigh-way... repudiates any suggestion of a hierarchy, such as the one Plato offers in *The Republic*, in which some kinds of information can properly be called knowledge while others are mere facts, and still others are only opinion. In such a world, the database itself supplies no standards for judging one piece of information superior to or more useful than another. Indeed, in such a world, standards cease to matter. Information itself becomes background noise, like the constantly running tap that television has already become.[7]

'Data networks contain facts by the billion', McGrath concluded. 'They do not provide meanings.' So how are we to find meaning in all this information? In *The Observer*, Naughton suggested using a 'cyberhound': software which functions as 'an intelligent agent', sifting through the data stream in search of the nuggets of information which are valuable to you personally. However, all this does is collect the fragments and make them more usable in their own terms. Convenient, yes; but no answer to the substantive problem of how to measure the fragments and piece them together into a broader framework.

Saul Wurman, described by Keegan as 'the US guru who coined the phrase "information anxiety"', warns that 'the greatest crisis facing modern civilisation is going to be how to transform information into structured knowledge. Society faces an over-abundance of data that needs to be evaluated and acted upon.'[8]

Wurman seems to be suggesting that information can somehow be worked up into a system of knowledge. But how? Information only becomes the raw material of knowledge when it is connected together by means of a conceptual (not technical) framework. Moreover, the existence of such a framework depends on society as a whole. The absence of this framework cannot be compensated for by improved search engines and more sophisticated new media, because the current absence of a coherent worldview was never the product of software or new media in the first place. Indeed, the undifferentiated character of incoherent information was perceived as a problem long before the advent of the Internet; and in the mid-seventies when film director Nicholas

Roeg (*The Man Who Fell to Earth*) wanted to show his protagonist (David Bowie) suffering from information overload, he sat him down in front of a bank monochrome television sets.

Information overload and information mania are both derived not from the rise of new technologies but from the collapse of Big Ideas. The structures which previously allowed information to become part of public knowledge were the 'metanarratives' and 'totalizing epistemologies' which have been rejected not only by postmodernists and deconstructionists, but by the rest of society as well, in the attempt to free ourselves from the allegedly repressive aspects of civilization. Relief from the pressure to organize experience according to a 'metanarrative' is one and the same thing as the stress of being exposed to undifferentiated data.

Play/work

In today's society, play and work represent two sides of the same culture of fear.

When a man's working life meant clocking in at the same time, same place for 40 odd years, and being given a clock as he walked through the factory gates for the last time aged 65, the distinction between work and play was simple enough. But the dividing line between the two has become much less distinct, especially in cyberculture.

The blurring process is not entirely new, however. In fifties America, when the bulk of work in Western countries started to shift towards white-collar employees in the service sector, a new model of company-oriented leisure arose simultaneously. Whereas most male workers would previously have spent most of their non-working time in the company of other men living nearby, perhaps in pool halls like those described by Ned Polsky in his account of their postwar decline,[1] in the fifties a growing proportion of men either spent more leisure time with company clients and colleagues, or they brought their work home with them in the shape of the boss and his wife who came to dinner. This was the apogee of corporate culture. At the time there was widespread concern that company life was taking over people's whole existence and turning them into carbon copies of each other – 'the organization man'.

In the sixties and seventies, the emphasis was entirely different. Among some of the most influential sections of society, the Protestant work ethic was discredited along with mainstream politics and the idea of progress. People began to define themselves more in terms of their leisure than their work (this was the period in which the term 'lifestyle' first came into use). Furthermore, there was an attempt on the part of a minority to transform work into a productive form of play. This occurred mainly within the confines of the counterculture, and was reflected in the new-found popularity of Johan Huizinga's book on man-the-player, *Homo Ludens*,[2] in preference to *homo sapiens* (rational or,

literally, wise man) or *homo faber* (man-the-manufacturer).
Similar ideas were expressed in a more hippie-friendly fash-
ion in a book entitled *Playpower* by Richard Neville, the
Australian editor of the underground magazine *Oz*.[3]

In the sixties the idea that work might be a form of personal
expression as much as a meal ticket or a socially useful function, affected only a mainly middle-class minority. But not long
afterwards such notions moved into wider circulation.

In some ways the eighties were a reaction against the sixties.
But in other respects they were a continuation. At a time of
recession, the faux poverty of the hippies seemed far less
attractive. It was time to go to work; but work, at this time,
was subject to redefinition. Jobs stopped being for life. Work
ceased to be for the common good; there was, after all, no such
thing as society. Instead there was money to be made and
pleasure to be taken – inside as well as outside office hours.
Lunch was for wimps and work was the new rock'n'roll.

The entrepreneurial eighties and the countercultural sixties came together in Silicon Valley, California, where this
unlikely sounding convergence was witnessd by author and
high-tech worker Dennis Hayes. In *Behind the Silicon Curtain:
The Seductions of Work in a Lonely Era*, Hayes combined repor-
tage and analysis in describing the insidious attractions of
working in a young and highly profitable industry where
labour was perceived as an extension of play:

> But the addictive kick for many computer workers is pre-
> cisely the intuitive, creative and emotional states they
> achieve at their terminals.
>
> 'Rapture. Epiphany', insists Michael, a systems utilities
> programmer who claims that 'the high that I'm getting out
> of it has very little to do with working with computers per
> se, but ... with the kind of problems. I'd say it's really very
> creative.'
>
> 'A feeling of total absorption. A feeling of, like, oblivion',
> says Victor, also a systems programmer. 'I used to do drugs
> a lot, when I was in college. And when I started working
> with computers, my drug use was cut drastically.'[4]

The suggestion here is that the world of work has taken on
some of the characteristics of the counterculture in that it can
often make the worker feel high. Hayes went on to explain

how in their leisure time the workers of Silicon Valley not only maintained the habits and expectations which they had picked up from the counterculture, but at the same time mimicked the tight deadlines and other pressures associated with the volatile computer industry:

> With the compulsiveness – and with many of the symptoms – of a drug habit, Silicon Valley imbues its free time with the fury and excess of work. Work is a port in the storm of life's uncertainties, because no matter how harrowing, work offers meaning (career logic, technical sophistication) and, for some, an escape from loneliness. The price of battening down all of social life to stay at work, however, is both dear and widely unchallenged. The positive and negative poles of work's magnetism are evident in work's resurgent popularity, and in the tripling in claims for work-induced stress in the 'Work Decade'. Self-conscious about leisure's instrumental role in sustaining work, Silicon Valley takes it in concentrated doses – partly because work and traffic jams compress free time, but also because the collective appetite for relief is apparently insatiable. If shopping relieves boredom and exercise eases stress, then the intensity with which Silicon Valley shops and exercises indicates intolerable boredom and debilitating stress. As individuals burden play with the utilitarian mission of relieving anxiety, play crosses the threshold into therapy (and becomes less playful).[5]

Hayes described a situation in which large numbers of employees who felt somehow vulnerable in their personal lives looked increasingly to work as the sphere of activity in which to ground themselves. But the world of work proved equally unstable, and their role in it turned out to be as contingent and fragmented as their personal lives. So they transferred their nervous energy into the sphere of personal consumption, which in turn had the effect of making their personal lives feel hyper-fragile; and so the spiral of fear continued to grow.

In one sense this process is simply a continuation of the way in which our work and our leisure are mirror images of each other. But what are the core notions which they both reflect, and are these notions subject to change?

In the nineteenth century, the Protestant work ethic in the factory and what have subsequently become known as family values in the home came together as mutually reinforcing elements of the widespread belief that the best of all possible worlds, if not here already, would not be too long in coming. But such confidence is utterly out of place in the nervous nineties. As described by Hayes, the mood in Silicon Valley arose from an unprecedented lack of confidence which was then expressed in both work and play.

In amongst all this nervousness, the worker can feel neither fully confident about his labour nor fully relaxed when ostensibly at ease. Leisure becomes almost a chore designed to improve performance at work; meanwhile work has to be redesigned to resemble a game or else no one will take it seriously. The result is a farcical remake of the interlocking elements of nineteenth-century self-confidence, except that this time around the complementary aspects are strongly indicative of self-doubt on a societal scale.

The nineties have been characterized by an attempt to escape from what is now regarded as the over-intensity of the eighties – the latter epitomized by the construction of high-tech 'campuses' staffed by college leavers who were encouraged to live and work together in a hothouse atmosphere. Nowadays going for the burn is as unfashionable as 'slash and burn' sackings and other forms of eighties-style 'downsizing'.

The key word of the nineties is 'downshifting', which often means giving up a high-pressure job in the inner city for a more 'sustainable' way of life in the country. But even here there is no respite. In 'telecottages' which are geographically distanced from urban connotations and the pressures associated with them, no one dares to turn the phone off or leave e-mail unread overnight in case there is a message from one of the teleworker's many bosses demanding extra work that needs to have been done yesterday.

Work and leisure have not become entirely indistinguishable, as some critics have erroneously claimed, but in the late eighties and nineties they have both been reformulated as part of the contemporary culture of fear.

Queer/ordinary

Nowadays being queer is less than extraordinary.

Back in November 1994, Steve Silberman, author of *Skeleton Key: A Dictionary for Deadheads*, wrote an article for *Wired* about queer teens who were finding solace and self-expression online. 'Now online interaction lets teens find other gay youngsters – as well as mentors', Silberman wrote. His piece focused on the liberatory experiences of one John Teen O, who identified with Franz Kafka's insect-man Gregor Samsa and was prone to bouts of suicidal depression until he started to meet other young queers in their own dedicated newsgroups.

Silberman painted a picture of gays besieged in their homes, colleges and workplaces by mainstream society and its homophobia. But is this still the case? It is certainly true that the hitlist of dangerous computer porn circulated by the Metropolitan Police in the summer of 1996 included some sites that could only have been considered dangerous because they dealt with gay sex. Furthermore, Internet service providers are still extremely wary of any gay site that appears to encourage particpation by anyone under the legal age of consent. However, in a more important respect, upholders of the queer sensibility can feel fully at home in cyberculture. This is because large tracts of cyberspace and the people who inhabit them conform to the notion of 'failed seriousness' coined in the early sixties by the American critic Susan Sontag in her brilliant description of the Camp sensibility, which at the time was closely associated with homosexual subcultures.[1]

Sontag attempted to identify the constituent elements of Camp, and she concluded that the precondition for Camp was an orientation to the world of 'failed seriousness', which in turn was reflected in the objects and icons chosen and collected by Camp-followers. But what was then the sensibility of a mainly homosexual minority has subsequently gone mainstream. Indeed if 'failed seriousness' remains a viable definition, then cyberculture almost in its entirety could be said to be Camp.

In the rest of the world also, being gay is nowhere near as queer as it was. The closing sequence of the fashionable BBC drama series *This Life* featured a gay couple smooching romantically on the dance floor while all around them heterosexual couples were bickering and lying to each other: the effect was to advertise gay relationships as an improvement on their heterosexual counterparts. Likewise the accolades dished out to Stephen Fry in 1997 are indicative of the relative normalization of being gay. Fry qualifies as Camp by being first of all a celebrity failure (a comedian who walked out on a West End show because he could not cope with it) who is now taking on serious roles like that of Oscar Wilde in the eponymous film. At the time of its release, the film's screenwriter Julian Mitchell tried to claim that Wilde was a rebel figure whose sexuality still poses a threat to British society a hundred years later. But this claim seems at odds with a society in which cabinet members can be 'out' and the government sends messages of support to Gay Pride.

It would be marvellous if the normalization of queer meant the full of extension of equal rights to all lesbians and gays who had previously been oppressed. In fact there is a process of equalization at work here, but it is of a different order. In the diffusion of the outlook of 'failed seriousness' across cyberspace and throughout society, there is an expectation that all of us should expect to be limited by the same constraints that were formerly applied only to oppressed groups such as homosexuals: we are all 'poofs' now. The invitation, therefore, is not to equal rights but to an equality of degradation, in which being gay is okay but only because the alleged personal weaknesses with which it was particularly associated have now been projected onto society as a whole.

Risk/safety

At one and the same time, cyberspace is seen as a safe environment, and as a dangerous place to be.

From America's Al Gore and Bill Gates to Italy's Carlo de Benedetti and Japan's Masayoshi Son, dozens of academics, business leaders, and politicians have painted a detailed picture of the coming digital millennium. We'll work, shop, chat, educate and amuse ourselves in a new online realm that will put every conceivable form of information – from a stock report to a digitized, interactive movie – instantly at our fingertips. Already millions of people around the world who collaborate across computer networks or log on to commercial online services or prowl the vast Internet are seeing a glimmer of how the vision will come to life.

They're probably seeing something else as well: despite all the high speed networks and powerful PCs to take you there, cyberspace – especially the uncharted expanse known as the Internet – is still not a safe, hospitable, and compelling environment for businesses and consumers. Often, it seems a harsh and unforgiving place where, with a misplaced keystroke, you can become hopelessly lost, where the information you thought you would find isn't where it should be, and where it's all too easy for villains to snatch your digital valuables – by ripping off your work or stealing your credit-card information.

Business Week Special Report, 27 February 1995.

Only a couple of years ago cyberspace was heralded as the electronic playground where anything goes and everything is safe. Suddenly it carries almost as many sinister connotations as the inner city or the 'underclass'. The online world is divided into cyber-victims and cyber-predators. Utopian cyberbabble is all but drowned out by dystopian Net-lash (the backlash against the Internet). Citing a front-page piece in the *New York Times* which warned that 'college stu-

108

dents are getting sucked into endless hours of online activity',
an Associated Press piece about a man who went online
'to find someone to rape his wife', and the bizarre story of
the torture fetishist who advertised on the Internet for
someone to kill her, *Washington Post* staff reporter John
Schwartz observed that 'The Net has become the all-purpose
scary place, good for a quick headline or government initiative.'[1]

On the face of it, there is a yawning gap between naive
faith in the healing powers of the information superhighway,
and the cynicism which insists that human beings are destined to screw up in cyberspace just like they have messed up
everywhere else. But naivete and cynicism are two sides of
the same coin.

Naive enthusiasm for life in cyberspace is often an expression of pessimism about pre-existing society. Cyberbabble
usually represents a yearning to escape from the apparently
intractable problems of the off-line world into the virgin
territory of digital communications, untainted by the 'geek-
flesh' of human beings.

Likewise, cynicism about cyberspace is a symptom of the
excessive problematization of already existing society. Such a
low opinion of a new and as yet largely unexplored terrain
can only have been formed by negative perceptions of the
off-line world which we already know and love to hate. Both
strands, cyberbabble and Net-lash, are predicated on an
extremely negative view of humanity and an intensely apprehensive attitude towards society.

The negative assumptions which are common to both
cyberbabble and Net-lash are clearly demonstrated in the
stormy debate about cybersex.

In the early nineties, conference audiences across the Western world were delighted by the prospect of 'teledildonics'.
There was general amusement and even excitement at the
thought of sex in VR – with whoever you wanted, whenever
you wanted it. Writing in 1990, Howard Rheingold prophe-
sied that 'portable teledildonics systems' would be 'ubiquituous' in 30 years.[2] 'There is no reason', continued Rheingold,
'to believe you won't be able to map your genital effectors to
your manual sensors and have direct genital contact by shak-
ing hands'.

Today Rheingold's suggestion would be frowned upon, and the same conference audiences would almost certainly condemn such enthusiasm as tasteless and irresponsible. Nowadays the playfully Camp neologism 'teledildonics' is rarely heard in respectable company. It has been superseded by terms such as 'cyber-stalking' which are pregnant with high moral tone. Mere mention of cybersex prompts ritual expressions of contempt for the likes of Jake Baker, the 20-year-old Michigan student arrested by the FBI in 1995 for alleged 'cyber-rape' after posting a torture and murder fantasy which referred to one of his classmates by name (charges against Baker were later dropped).

The discrepancy between the euphoria and the fear surrounding cybersex is by no means as great as it seems. Indeed they are united by a common preoccupation with safety.

The euphoric response to the idea of cybersex was at least partly derived from the assumption that old-fashioned sexual contact is inherently unsafe, in that it generally entails the exchange of bodily fluids and the ensuing possibility of sexually transmitted disease. Cybersex, however, entails neither. The digital world offers a sealed environment, a prophylactic against physical leakage. Thus cybersex was welcomed as a new form of safe sex, and the safety factor inherent in it was always the main attraction.

In a magazine feature entitled 'Sitting Naked At The Keyboard',[3] a representative of the cybersex site Wank Central (http://www.paranoia/com/~macb3th/nycu) confirmed this observation when he spoke to journalist Cotton Ward about the disadvantages and the advantage of sharing sexual fantasies over the Internet:

> Anybody's who's tried on-line and physical sex will prefer real-life sex, just for the physical and emotional intimacy. A disadvantage of Net sex is getting 'desynched'... an example of this is when a person does something to you that would require you to be sitting down, but by the time that message reaches you, you've already sent them a message indicating you're standing up. It can be quite annoying and interrupt the fantasy. The huge advantage of on-line sex is that it's completely safe.

But can safe sex ever be safe enough? The experience of cybersex suggests not. For all its immunity to physical penetration, the online world offers no protection against ideological intercourse. Regardless of the technical properties of digital communications, the widespread association of sex with risk made its way into cyberspace willy-nilly; and loose talk of 'teledildonics' was quickly subsumed into the wider discussion of sexual victims, addicts and predators. Thus the idea of cybersex as anonymous, harmless and playful was soon replaced by notions of cybersex as dangerous, manipulative and intrusive.

The transformation of safe-cybersex into an allegedly risky business is a vivid example of the spiral of apprehension which characterizes society today. The more safety is sought after, the more it becomes impossible to achieve; and the more we tend to be overwhelmed by a sense of being vulnerable and at risk.

The sense of being at risk is the defining feature of Hollywood's representation of cyberculture. It also features prominently in novels set in and around cyberspace. In 'Slash And Backlash', an article in the UK edition of *Wired*,[4] journalist Jim McClellan observed that 'in this age of cultural hybrdids and gen(r)e splicing', film-makers and novelists are keen to 'mix and match the two foremost modern bogey men – the serial killer and the irresponsible hacker'. McClellan cited movies such as Rachel Tallaly's *Ghost in the Machine* (1993; featuring 'a serial killer morphed onto the Net'); Brett Leonard's *Virtuosity* (1995; featuring 'Sid 6.7, an evolving AI [artificial intelligence] that combined all history's great serial killers'); and *The Net* (1995), in which 'a Bill Gates clone and his dastardly English henchman stalk Sandra Bullock around LA'. His selection of cyber-victim novels included *Mother of God* by David Ambrose, in which 'a computer-genius-turned-serial-killer hooks up with a "conscious" AI that has escaped onto the Net and plans world domination'; Philip Finch's *F2F* – 'a Doom-damaged dweeb gets into a flame war on a WELL-style conferencing system and decides to waste everyone who aimed virtual vitriol his way'; and Philip Kerr's *Gridiron* – 'an AI gone bad turns an intelligent building into a self-organising house of horror'.

Putting them all together, McClellan reported the 'increasing prominence' of 'what you could call the net-stalker genre, in which hapless victims are terrorised by a hacking serial killer, or his digital surrogate, a malevolent computer that is part Hal, part Hannibal Lecter'. The genre, he noted, is characterized by 'Frankenstein-style moralising' which often takes the form of 'warnings about transgressing limits, usurping God and Nature', and sometimes includes a slap on the wrists for those who have been 'informationally loose' – for example, by leaving their computer and modems switched on all night, they have left themselves open to abuse by cyber-predators. McClellan concluded that in this new generation of horror,

> the thing that comes back to haunt us in net-stalker fiction is our own networked lives (and our lack of control over them), the way we're all enmeshed in a global digital web, the way our informational selves are just lying there, alone and vulnerable.

In other words, the new fiction paints a picture of the risks which are now seen as inherent in the one place we thought we could be safe – cyberspace.

Concern about 'net-stalking' is by no means confined to the world of fiction. In *The Guardian* Online supplement, Joia Shillingford warned that if you 'send personal data on the Net', you 'could be at risk from cyberterrorists'. In an article headlined 'The Ugly Facts at your Fingertips',[5] Shillingford first explained that digital information can easily find its way into the wrong hands; and then went on to quote 'security architect' Tom Parker, who claimed that 'it is very dangerous to send out any personal data over the Net' unless it is encoded in advanced encryption software.

Again, the very search for safety seems to have added to the sense of being at risk. Many users of the Internet moved into cyberspace because it seemed less threatening than the world beyond the computer room. One of the attractions of online shopping, for example, is that the virtual mall is impenetrable to the hooded muggers who are alleged to lurk in the dark places of urban shopping centres. But now it seems that putting oneself on the Internet leaves one more exposed than ever before.

Parents concerned about the safety of their children are facing the same sort of conundrum. Filled with apprehension about the alleged dangers outside the home, some parents have opted to keep their kids off the streets and in front of the computer, only to be told that they may be exposing their children to the dangers of cyberporn, and the possibility of being approached online by paedophiles. So the parents duly install some kind of safety software which prevents their kids accessing unsuitable material. But then they are told that the mere experience of being on the Internet – regardless of the material that is being accessed – may be addictive, and therefore detrimental to the health of people in general and children in particular. Whatever they do, the risks keep on coming, to the point where safety becomes the Holy Grail of the nervous nineties.

The spontaneously reproducing spiral of 'risk consciousness' leads us to live our lives in ever-decreasing circles. Far from being immune from this debilitating process, cyberculture is one of the arenas where it is most clearly expressed.

Subject/object

In cyberculture the objectification of social change obliterates the historical subject.

The term 'cyberpunk' is an oxymoron, that is, the two elements which go to make up this word are mutually exclusive, and their proximity is therefore sharply ('oxy') foolish ('moron'). But unpacking this foolishness may help to formulate some sensible insights into the contradictions of cyberculture and the society which it describes.

The prefix 'cyber', as in cyberculture, is taken from the Ancient Greek word meaning 'pilot'. It connotes an individual with a definite destination in mind and a planned route for getting there. It may also imply a heroic struggle against the tide. Above all, it suggests an individual who is acting upon the external world, rather than being acted upon. Writ large, this would serve as an approximate definition of the historical subject. Characters from modern literature who fit this description include Shelley's *Prometheus Unbound* and the problem-solving protagonist of the detective novel in its initial form.

The suffix 'punk' means quite the opposite. Originally used to describe the passive partner in a homosexual relationship, it gradually became a general term for youngsters who had already been marked down as losers. Then in the seventies it was adopted by a new generation of youth who saw themselves as having been brutalized and disfigured by society; and who sought to re-present their disfigurement back to the society which caused it. The common element in all three usages is the notion of the individual as primarily the recipient of external pressures. Instead of acting upon the world, this individual is defined by the extent to which he is an object that is acted upon.

The term 'cyberpunk' encapsulates the degradation of the heroic subject into the objectified cultural personality of today. In its internal contradictions, 'cyberpunk' is an appropriate emblem for a culture which is deliberately directionless, and symbolic of the self-made society which has lost its sense of steerage way.

In cyberpunk fiction, the protagonists tend to be both threatened and propelled by external elements which have somehow impregnated them and got under their skin. They are driven, rather than hard-driving. In William Gibson's *Johnny Mnemonic*, for example, the personal identity of the eponymous protagonist is under threat from the data which he carries in his head on behalf of corporate clients. Likewise, in *Neuromancer*,[1] the anti-hero Case is desperately trying to escape the effects of the toxins implanted in his own arteries. Both stories give the impression of the self under siege in today's world. This was certainly the interpretation placed upon Gibson's *Johnny Mnemonic* by the man who directed the film version, Robert Longo. In the press pack issued with the film, Longo is quoted as saying: 'We all have to be very careful not to lose ourselves, our humanness, in this age of information and speed.'[2]

But if some of Gibson's leading characters are in danger of being re-programmed by corporate gangsters, others are already pre-programmed by their own fixed personalities. In *Cyberia: Life in the Trenches of Hyperspace*, Douglas Rushkoff noted that cyberpunk's 'characters must behave absolutely true to their programming, having no choice but to follow the instructions of their emotional templates. Even Molly, the closest thing to a love-interest in *Neuromancer*, leaves her boyfriend with a written, self-defeating apology: '"it's the way I'm wired I guess".'[3] With such characters, Gibson returns to the pre-modern notion of pre-determined personal destiny. Whether or not they escape from a fate worse than death, Gibsonian protagonists are fated to behave in certain ways. In this respect, Gibson's work has more in common with *Prometheus Bound* by Aeschylus than with Shelley's *Prometheus Unbound*. Like Greek tragedy, and unlike the literature of the Enlightenment, it suggests that the scope for rational choice in human activity is extremely limited.

Pat Cadigan, described by fellow feminist sci fi writer Gwyneth Jones as 'the only woman in the original cadre' of cyberpunk, also creates characters who 'do not act, they react' to what is done to them. Of the female protagonists of Cadigan's *Mindplayers and Fools*, Jones has said that 'they may be on the street; they certainly aren't in control'; and that they are 'too wise to contest with their menfolk for the centre stage'.[4] In re-defining 'wise' as the decision not to engage, Jones is reflecting the current antipathy towards contestation, and thereby contributing to the consequent diminution of the historical subject. Indeed she welcomes this latter as 'the downsizing (or rightsizing) of self', which is 'inescapably a political, and a feminist progress'.[5] If so, then feminism must be the politics of self-degradation, and 'progress' has already been transformed into its opposite.

Gibson's characters come dressed in black leather jackets, while the protagonists of sci fi feminism tend to look like Courtney Love in cyberspace. In their presentational form, they are the epitome of cool. But in their essentially passive relationship to the world in motion around them, they are more like nerds. Then again, in resigning from history and celebrating the individual's dislocation from society, perhaps the cult of the cool always did point towards nerdishness. Each is a self-caricaturing response to the twentieth-century impasse; and both of these self-images presage the obliteration of the historical subject. Indeed they may have already come together in the Japanese cult of Otaku, the highly fashion-conscious young people who prefer pre-set gadgets to unpredictable people.

These trends are not confined to the fictional realms of cyberculture. Some of the foremost champions of cyberculture have formulated an equally passive image of themselves – and the rest of us – in relation to the alleged inevitability of technological change and its social implications. Asked by Mark Slouka whether life in cyberspace would be advantageous to humanity, John Perry Barlow, co-founder of the Electronic Frontier Foundation, replied that there would be 'damned few' advantages, but there was nothing we could do about it. 'Advantage has nothing to do with it. There are many evolutionary forces at work here, most of them working against us. All of them inexorable.'[6]

When pressed by Slouka on the business of 'leaving the flesh behind' and 'uploading ourselves into the Net', Barlow retreated even further into fatalism:

Again, it's less a matter of advantage than inevitability. It's happening and will continue to. If I could stop it I would... But when you're about to be swept over the falls, you might as well try to enjoy the ride.[7]

Cyberculture is generally sympathetic to the notion that all we can do is 'go with the flow'. Many Netizens evince a kind of noisy quietism, in which they shout loudly about the low volume of the human potential. Statements along the following lines are commonplace:

> Cyberpunk is dealing with a dysfunctional world – a world which we didn't make and one that we aren't going to fix. It's not that we don't *want* to fix it. We would, if we could, but we can't, so we won't. Nothing can fix this world... We are all headed for oblivion but some of us want to have our eyes open.[8]

Through the prism of such defeatism, the term 'cultural revolution', which is often used in connection with cyberspace, no longer connotes social transformation at the hands of human agents but comes to mean the spontaneous realization of a cyclical pattern. Political 'activism' is translated as pranksterism that will 'tickle the funny bone' of society. In a similar vein John Perry Barlow has advocated an an ontology of impotence, which he describes as 'the learning curve of Sisyphus', and an epistemology of confusion: 'Once you start to embrace confusion as a way of life, concomitant with that is the assumption that you really don't control anything. At best it's a matter of surfing the whitewater.'[9]

Refusing to go with the flow is dubbed 'neurotic' by Barlow. Likewise, cyberfeminist Sadie Plant appeared to dismiss rationality as the mark of an unbalanced individual: 'By the end of the twentieth century only the most one-track, fixated, single-minded individuals continued to think that focus and concentration worked.'[10]

For these commentators technology is now the subject, and the real subject of history – humanity – is therefore object-ified. This means, in turn, that their notion of social change is at once exaggerated and truncated. Kevin Kelly, the co-founder of *Wired* magazine, naturalizes human history in the suggestion that a new generation of machines is going back to nature and taking us along with it. In an interview which coincided with the publication of his influential book

Out of Control: The New Biology of Machines, Kelly opined that 'As we make machines more complicated, their level of complexity approaches that of living organisms and systems such as a butterfly or tundra. Machines and living organisms are really two sides of the same coin.'[11] By the same token, the conscious human activity which has resulted in the manufacture of computers is subsumed within the unconscious process of evolution:

> The book at one time was subtitled The Rise of Artificial Evolution. What it was trying to do was recast evolution; take it from being the quintessential biological thought, and show that it can be moved into computers.[12]

More recently, Kelly has tried to take political economy down the same retrograde path. In an extensive article for *Wired* magazine entitled 'New Rules for the New Economy', he claimed that 'wasting time and being inefficient are the way to discovery', and concluded by reformulating the idea of going with the flow into the following instruction: 'In the Network Economy, don't solve problems, seek opportunities.'[13]

The outlook shared by many cyberculturists tends to deny human subjectivity and to project it onto digital technology, which is, like all technologies, only the lifeless product of human activity which is then used to facilitate further human activity. Thus R.U. Sirius told Douglas Rushkoff that *Mondo 2000* promotes social change without being attached to particular causes;[14] from being a focused, instrumental dynamic arising out of conscious activity, change has here been recast as an arbitrary movement led, presumably, by the autonomous energy of technology. Similarly, Gwyneth Jones suggests that 'the multitudinous immaterial presence' of the Internet is 'perhaps the nearest thing to an alien intelligence we'll ever meet'.[15] While the Internet is endowed with the characteristics of human activity, it is surely no coincidence that the abbreviated term by which it is widely known, 'the Net', connotes human beings not only connected with each other, but also trapped within the confines of a net. Thus technology takes on the appearance of an open-ended entity in its own right, and humanity's lot is seen as circumscribed and objectified.

The objectification of human history is by no means the same as objectivity. On the contrary, it thrives on the kind of internalized, highly individuated subjectivity which might best be described as subjectivism. This is subjectivity reduced to the level of personal perception and prejudice – that is, it has not been tempered in the attempt to change the external world or tested in an effort to analyse society objectively.

Antipathy to objectivity is expressed in the growing emphasis on fiction and literary criticism (a loose-knit sphere which can never be entirely free from the personal prejudices of the critic any more than it can dispense with the imagination of the author). With its close definitions and more rigorous methods, scientific analysis is increasingly unwelcome. But both science and literature have been degraded to the extent that today they hardly exist as distinct spheres of intellectual activity. Under the rubric of 'culture', fiction and its appreciation are now held up as the cutting edge of sociology. Novels are what passes for the new social critique.

At the Governance of Cyberspace conference in April 1995, Roger Burrows from the University of Teesside presented a paper which analysed 'the emergence of cyberpunk as social theory', and in which he observed that various critics have also 'begun to treat the cyberpunk literature as an analytic resource which can be utilised in the service of social theory'.[16]

Burrows is attached to the Centre for the Study of Adult Life, but what he is describing sounds like the infantilization of social theory. Under the heading 'recursivity', he cites Doug Kellner's call for the blurring of the lines between social science and science fiction:

> Cyberpunk science fiction can be read as a sort of social theory, while Baudrillard's futuristic postmodern social theory can be read in turn as science fiction. This optic also suggests a deconstruction of sharp oppositions between literature and social theory, showing that much social theory contains a narrative and vision of the present and future, and that certain types of literature provide cogent mappings of the contemporary environment and, in the case of cyberpunk, of future trends... At the very moment when Baudrillard dropped the theoretical ball,

losing his initiative, Gibson and cyberpunk picked it up, beginning their explorations of the new future world which Baudrillard had been exploring.[17]

Along similar lines, Mike Davis, whose book on Los Angeles: *City of Quartz*, provides many well-researched insights into contemporary society, nevertheless seems to be advocating the dumbing-down of social criticism by suggesting that the novels of William Gibson can provide the basis for both understanding and changing society. Davis describes Gibson's stories as 'stunning examples of how realist "extrapolative" science fiction can operate as prefigurative social theory, as well as an anticipatory opposition politics to the cyber-fascism lurking over the next horizon'.[18] (But perhaps we should not be surprised by this from a man who once told me that he used to try to identify factory workers who might join the vanguard of the working-class revolution according to whether or not they owned any records by avant-garde black musicians.)

If all that was being said was that fiction is often highly illustrative of the historical context from which it is derived, this would be unexceptionable. But the inflated claim being made for cyberpunk (not by the cyberpunks themselves, it should be noted) is that it is analytical, theoretical, and political. This is not only a gross underestimation of the pre-conditions for social criticism; it also creates confusion which in turn hinders the development of clear analysis, coherent theory and cutting-edge politics.

Such trends have been much in evidence at the annual Virtual Futures conferences hosted by Nick Land of the philosophy department at Warwick University – one of those events where the term 'interdisciplinary' is a euphemism for the absence of any intellectual discipline at all. At Virtual Futures, postgrad students read their papers as if they were poems (some of them are certainly more poetic than rational), and top-flight cybernauts talk about whatever they feel like talking about. At one of the conferences which I attended, Manuel De Landa presented his theory of 'stratification', which holds that physical and social processes alike are made up of 'sorting out' and 'consolidation':[19] geological rock formations and human society, they work the same way.

De Landa seems to want to degrade theory still further. He has suggested that its future lies in the 'epistemiological reservoirs' drawn from computer simulations of various aspects of society.[20] Burrows adds: 'those of us familiar with the analytic insights simulations such as Sim City 2000 can afford will have had a small glimpse of the sort of thing De Landa has in mind'.[21] So now 'theory' not only encompasses the writing and reading of fiction, it also includes devising and playing sophisticated computer games. In short, theory is whatever you want it to be.

Those who are amazed that this is where social theory has got to at the end of the twentieth century may care to recall that, even its early, Weberian incarnation, sociology was developed as the means to understand society 'objectively' while at the same time screening out the possibility of open-ended human agency, at that time represented by the working class as a political entity. Yet there can be no objectivity which does not take account of the historical subject, and vice versa. In cyberculture, subjectivism and its corollary, the objectification of social change, bear witness to the interdependence of subjectivity and objectivity. It is unfortunate that this relationship is currently expressed in the degradation of both parties rather than their elevation.

Technical/cultural

If cyberculture is not defined by the technologies
employed in it, is it determined by anything at all?

What was expected to be a centralizing, unifying factor is
now, thirtysomething years later, widely interpeted as an
agent of decentralization and fragmentation. The constant
element in these vastly different expectations is computer
technology, which in the sixties seemed to be an important
addition to the mode of communications known as broadcasting, and is now seen as the cutting edge of 'narrowcasting'. Same, or similar, technology; applied differently in
society at various times.

From this it can be seen that technical explanations of
cyberculture will never be sufficient. Not even bricks and
mortar are immune to social change. Journalist Julia Thrift
has explained how seaside bungalows were built in the
first half of the twentieth century to accommodate a new
generation of bohemians on the run from urban conformity,
only to be squatted by the next cohort of emigrants
from the city – the suburban middle classes whose *modus
vivendi* was a byword in anti-bohemian respectability.[1]
Like domestic space, cyberspace and the manner of its technical construction are entirely subject to historical developments.

This is not to say, however, that the technical characteristics
of cyberspace are irrelevant. An important factor in the
spread of the Internet is the unique technical facility for
many-to-many communication. Likewise, the replicability
that comes with digital technology is the *sine qua non* of online
networking. But technological capability does not create
demand *per se* (look at what happened to quadrophonic
sound); rather, communications technologies are regarded
as successful when they fulfil needs which already exist,
embryonically perhaps, in society. Thus the 'de-centred'
Internet has come to the fore at a time when our lives have
become more diffuse. Cyberspace and its attendant technologies constitute the medium which is most appropriate for

our times. They are society's messenger-boy; never the message.

So how are we to understand the domination of society over technology? Many of those opposed to the techno-determinist approach seek to explain the subordination of technology in cultural terms; indeed the common usage of the term 'cyberculture' is indicative of this trend. But the trend, if not the term itself, is problematic.

Proponents of cultural explanations often refer to the definition of culture offered by the late Raymond Williams. In *The Long Revolution*, Williams wrote that culture

> is a description of a particular way of life, which expresses certain meanings and values not only in art and learning but in institutions and ordinary behaviour. The analysis of culture, from such a definition, is the clarification of the meanings and values implicit and explicit in a particular way of life, a particular culture.[2]

Williams was careful to say that culture is a 'description' of a way of life, which suggests that there is something there first for culture to describe. Those who refer to Williams' definition of culture, however, often re-write it so as to suggest that culture *is* a way of life, in its entirety. In their usage, representation and reality are indistinguishable; and 'culture' becomes a catch-all term which includes everything without differentiating between determining factors and those elements which are determined by them. It therefore contains everything and explains nothing.

Moreover, this is to obstruct the use of 'culture' as a category with which to analyse how a society describes itself. Indeed in its current usage, analysis is superseded by mere description, as I tried to explain in an essay on the notion of crime as culture:

> At best this is a description of crime as an activity which individuals learn from social interaction. Of course it is true that each criminal does not invent crime anew. John Donne's observation that 'no man is an island' applies as much to the lawbreaker as to the poet who hears the funeral bell. But why should there be a propensity to learn crime rather than, say, hard work and self-discipline? The description of

crime as culture offers no explanations for this. It stalls at the level of surface appearances, yet it is often advanced as if it were the last word in penetrating analysis'.[3]

Those who use the term 'culture' in this way are often as oblivious as techno-determinists to the real process of social change. Either 'culture' is seen as something habitual, closed and fixed, or it is regarded as entirely fluid, open-ended and voluntary. In each version, social determinants are noticeable by their absence. Both definitions tend to promote an objectified notion of culture (either resistant to change or itself the expression of objectified change), which in its proximity to the biological usage of the term suggests a degraded view of human society as something akin to an organic growth.

Both technology and culture are formulated and reformulated according to the trajectory of historical change as it occurs in society. Understanding the process of historical change requires a critique of society which looks at our activity as a totality, while at the same time isolating the fundamental relationships which are most important and identifying the mediations through which their influence is brought to bear, all the way up to the level of surface appearances.

Neither technical nor cultural explanations are up to the job.

Universal/particular

You can see the world from cyberspace. But most people only go looking for themselves.

Many Netizens will admit to having had a magical, near-orgasmic experience when they first came online. Being directly in touch with other people in another part of the world, being able to see and interact with their online representation of themselves, has been known to prompt an adrenaline rush alongside feelings of warmth and empathy – a marvellous combination of responses which has largely eluded the counterculture in 50 years of searching for just this sort of high.

But the 'one world' feeling seems to operate according to a law of diminishing returns. Each time the Netizen goes online, the more the experience tends to become unexceptional. The same goes for the Internet industry as a whole. Already it has recognised that the experience of simply being on the Internet is no longer a marketable commodity. Increasingly, the industry is concerned with the content of what's online, rather than trying to sell the novelty of just being there.

Some commentators have referred to this process as 'desensitization', and inferred that we should feel a little bit guilty for allowing ourselves to become jaded so quickly. But how else could it be?

The initial moment of online joy is surely an expression of the desire in each and every one of us to escape our mutual alienation and reconnect with each other. This in turn is a reflection of the universalizing potential of the modern world – a world which is already connected, albeit indirectly, through the global market; and which carries within it the capacity to transcend itself by putting all of its people into a direct and creative relationship with each other.

However, this potential is continually stifled by the particular historical form of the society in which we live – a society which prevents productive cooperation among the majority except when such cooperation profits a privileged minority;

and which, as a consequence, also tends to promote atomization and individuation. Our experience of the Internet cannot help but be shaped by this contradiction. So it is that the
more being online becomes part of everyday experience as
lived in our anti-social society, the more its universalizing
potential tends to be obscured, and even forgotten entirely.

Furthermore, the 'one world' feeling is not unique to
the Internet. In the postwar period, it was thought that
television would promote a sense of interconnectedness. 'Television offers the soundest basis for world peace that has yet
been presented', declared *Scientific American* in June 1954.
'Peace must be created on the bulwark of understanding.
International television will knit together the peoples of the
world in bonds of mutual respect; its possibilities are vast,
indeed.'[1]

Likewise, in the first half of the twentieth century, the
development of the telephone network provoked a similar
response. My father, who was brought up in rural Oxford-
shire around the time of the First World War, recalls that
telephone users would preface their conversations by asking
'Are you there?' This question, which now seems absurdly
quaint, must have been redolent with the sort of wonderment
and naive pleasure which now surrounds our initial experiences online.

In each of these historical instances, the personal experience of the world in its interconnectedness has been a source
of joy, initially at least, to the individuals involved in it. But
none of these pleasurable experiences was simply the result
of the new technology which facilitated it. On the contrary,
the successive technologies involved were themselves dependent on the social relations which predated them.

Long before the TV or even the telephone, the world was
already 'wired' through the operation of the market (established in Europe and the United States of America in the first
half of the nineteenth century) and the international division
of labour (established by means of the externalizing dynamic
of imperialism towards the end of the nineteenth century).
On each occasion the connections which already existed as a
consequence of the social relations of production were intensified by the introduction of new technology. But in our anti-
social society, the intensification of our connectedness also

has the contradictory effect of further obscuring social relations and emphasizing our alienation.

The shift in the perceived role of television, from the expectation of social coherence and community-building in the fifties to the assumption that TV promotes atomization and 'couch potato' passivity in the nineties, bears witness to this contradiction. The culture surrounding the Internet, however, is the social/anti-social space where the contradiction between the universal and the particular finds its most intense expression.

It often happens that individuals go online with the avowed intention of opening themselves up to a new range of experiences. But, from the point of view of the particular individual, the sheer volume of postings on the Internet seems imponderable. So what can you do but scale down the range of sites you may consider visiting? And in this scaling down, what tends to get left out are those sites which do no reflect the interests and concerns which you already share. After all, you are not going to visit places which do not interest you when there is so much else out there, including stuff which fits your intellectual profile like a data glove.

In other words, the Netizen may set out to travel the digital world but the most popular route turns out to be the path to his own backyard. The circularity of this much-travelled route has been accurately described by M. Kadi, writing in the San Francisco-based 'zine *h2so4*:

J. Individual wants to join the online revolution, to connect and communicate. But J. is not going to read all one million posts on AOL... J. Individual is white. So J. Individual is going to ignore all the multicultural folders. J. couldn't give a hoot about gender issues and does not want to discuss religion or philosophy. Ultimately, J. Individual does not engage in topics that do not interest J. Individual. So who is J. meeting? Why, people who are *just like* J.

J. Individual has now... travelled the information highway and, just a few miles down that great democratic expressway, J. Individual has settled into an electronic suburb.

Are any of us so very different?... Oh yeah; I am so

connected, so enlightened, so open to the opposing viewpoint. I'm out there meeting people from different economic backgrounds (who have $120 a month to burn),
from all religions (yeah, right, like anyone actually dis-
cusses religion anymore from a user standpoint), from all
kinds of different ethnic backgrounds and with all kinds of
sexual orientations (as if any of this ever comes up outside
of the appropriate topic folder).

People are drawn to topics and folders that interest them
and therefore people will only meet people who are interested in the same topics in the same folders.[2]

If you can ignore the politically correct prejudices in her
article, Kadi seems to have done a good job in explaining
how the universal potential of the Internet tends to be
expressed in reverse, as a diminishing spiral of narrowing
concerns. So how could this particularist trend be turned into
its opposite? Kadi seems to think that it simply will not
happen, but she also gives the impression that, in the best
of all possible worlds, there might be some sort of moral
obligation to 'venture into a random folder just to see what
others (the Other?) are talking about'.[3]

In this formulation Kadi half-heartedly invites Netizens
to suspend their particular interests in favour of other people's, albeit temporarily. An unrealistic scenario if ever there
was one; and indeed it would be surprising if Kadi really
thought it would come about. This is not to say, however, that
there have never been circumstances in which people felt
the need to step beyond themselves and their particular
concerns.

Throughout history, there have been various instances in
which people from different backgrounds came together to
explore subjects of mutual interest which went way beyond
their personal frame of reference. But such exploration has
generally occurred in the collective attempt to realize a common cause. Whether that common cause was bourgeois progress or working-class revolution, the attempt to advance it,
and thereby improve the lot of humanity, prompted people
to put themselves in exceptional situations where they were
under pressure to expand their existing, personal knowledge
base. In such circumstances, whole generations of people did

indeed open the many 'folders' of human experience which were not relevant to them personally.

In each instance the sense of themselves as agents in history is what motivated people to carve out a trajectory between their own particular experience and the universal character of humanity. Moreover, by establishing a two-way path between the universal and the particular, they learnt to appreciate the true significance of each different element in the totality.

Today, however, we have no sense of ourselves as agents in history; and, as the Angry Young Man discovered in the fifties, 'there are no brave causes left'. More than 40 years on, the continuing absence of a pathway between the particular and the universal means that the latter now seems as impossible as the former is banal.

'Of course, it is not possible to be objective about the entire population, is it?', asked Internet commentator Melanie McGrath, rhetorically, in an interview coinciding with the publication of her highly-praised account of life online, *Hard, Soft and Wet: The Digital Generation Comes of Age*.[4] In fact the Internet facilitates just such a possibility; but while the culture surrounding the Internet continues along present lines, its universalizing potential will remain just that – a possibility. And we will find ourselves having to make do with 'differences', as McGrath has suggested.

I was very interested ... in the idea, much talked about on the West Coast of America, that there is such a thing as a global culture, a global village, and that technology can facilitate it. But I saw no sign of it at all. There is no consensus on what the Internet is for. In Singapore, for example, the Internet is a business tool and no one talks about virtual communities. But in Czechoslovakia the Net is seen primarily as a political tool, because it was so important in disseminating information in the Velvet Revolution. I think the differences between cultures should be celebrated, not squashed.

Indeed we should be recognising the particular variations in different cultures and localities, all the better to comprehend the universal themes which, by definition, are common to them all; and vice versa. With the advent of the Internet,

this relationship has never been easier to establish – technically. But with the fragmentation of society showing no signs
of abatement, the tendency to privilege the particular over
the universal has never been more pronounced; and cyberculture is crippled as a result.

Virtual reality/'virtual reality'

Enthusiasts look forward to immersion in virtual reality,
while some commentators have warned that we are
already in it.

In October 1992, *Business Week* introduced its readership to
the computer-generated worlds of virtual reality. A bevy of
staff writers was commissioned to dispel the 'confusion over
what VR is'. They explained that

> the core of every system is a data base . . . that can represent
> almost everything. A powerful computer with sophisticated
> graphics then renders a 'world', often in 3-D, that recreates
> precisely what the data describe . . . [T]wo characteristics
> distinguish VR worlds from other computer graphics:
> Increasingly, they convey multiple sensory information –
> sound or touch – to make environments more realistic.
> And they are interactive. In some systems, a viewer wear-
> ing a sensor-laden glove manipulates objects in the com-
> puter as one would naturally. In others, images on the
> screen or a viewer's perspective are manipulated with a
> mouse or a joystick.

This report was succinct and highly informative. But where
Business Week was straightforward and down to earth, other
commentators have been convoluted and extremely fanciful
about virtual reality (VR). In particular, the possibility of
being totally immersed in a VR system has been the cue for
all sorts of musings about the changing relationship between
perception and reality.

'Immersion' occurs when, in the mind's eye of the VR
user, the computer-generated environment takes precedence
over the real-life (RL) environment in which he is physically
situated. For this to happen, the VR environment must
be credible; not necessarily an exact representation of an
RL environment, but sufficiently representative of RL to
prompt the user to suspend disbelief. The relationship
between immersion and credibility was summarized by
Phil Judkins and Barrie Sherman, who led the first European

Commission inquiry into VR in the early nineties, in their
book about VR and its implications, *Glimpses of Heaven, Visions
of Hell*:

> The other factor is that users find the virtual world believe-
> able. Myron Kreuger [of the Artificial Reality Corporation],
> one of the ancients of this fledgling industry – he is old
> enough to remember John Kennedy at first hand – has
> what he calls 'the duck test'. If someone ducks away from a
> virtual stone aimed at their head, even if they know the
> stone is not real, it shows the world is believeable. This is
> known as 'immersion', and the aim of many VR practi-
> tioners is to achieve total immersion.[1]

In *The Guardian*, an enthusiastic Bob Swain described the
operation of VR and then declared that 'the distinction
between fact and fiction has already disappeared'.[2] Writing
in the *Daily Telegraph* about his first experience in virtual
reality, Eric Bailey was apprehensive. He reported that 'the
effect envelops your senses, until you forget that you are
wearing an ungainly helmet. You are a one-armed person
in a virtual world.'[3]

Bailey referred, ominously, to Aldous Huxley's *Brave New
World*: 'The VR experience is the closest experience yet to the
"feelies"...When it is no longer necessary to experience
reality, will the imagination, the ambition, the will to struggle
shrivel?'

Professor Michael Heim expressed similar qualms in *The
Metaphysics of Virtual Reality*. 'Will we', Heim asked, 'maintain
enough power of additional awareness needed for both primary and secondary worlds – at the same time?' Heim also
suggested that once immersed in virtual reality, we might
never be able to get back to reality as we have known it up
to now, because we will no longer be able to distinguish
between fact and digital fiction: 'We do not even realise
when we are trapped in our minds and cybersystems. The
basic world we incarnate gradually is lost in our attention to
the cognitive and imagined worlds.'[4]

Posing the question, 'how much can humans change and
still remain human as they enter the cyberspace of compu-
terised realities?', Heim warned that virtual reality presaged
'an ontological shift...a change in the world under our feet,

in the whole context in which our knowledge and awareness are rooted'.[5]

Dr William Bricken, principal scientist at the human interface technology laboratory, Seattle, also believes that VR is an epochal-development, both in technological and philosophical terms. Speaking in June 1991 at the first conference in Britain on VR, Bricken explained that virtual reality is inclusive; by placing 'the participant inside information', it shifts us 'from a feeling of viewing a picture to a feeling of being in a place...from being observers to having experiences, from interfacing with a display to inhabiting an environment'. But this technological innovation carried philosophical risks within it, Bricken warned. He mentioned 'cognitive remodelling', and admitted 'we don't have the faintest clue what is going on. We do not know the borders between the virtual and the actual.'

Bricken also predicted that the capacity to immerse ourselves in a fictional yet entirely convincing environment – what he described as 'immaterial realism' – would spell the end of 'Objectivism', which he defined as 'hundreds of years of favouritism for the objective, the scientific'. Other anticipated transformations included 'the shift from duality to pervasion...from networks to maps, from separation to unity, from confrontation to cooperation, from male to female, from one to zero'.[6]

For all his apocalyptic leanings, Bricken remains a champion of VR. Mark Slouka, on the other hand, is a committed opponent who includes virtual reality among the new 'school of technologies that threatens to permanently blur the line between what is real and what is not'; which in turn 'leads to a *political* reality as startling as it is ugly'.[7] In short, Slouka sees cyberspace as the location of 'the assault on reality', which is accompanied by 'the assault on place', 'the assault on community', and 'the assault on identity'.

This may sound a bit over the top; as indeed it is. Slouka, and for that matter Bricken *et al.*, seem to have overemphasized the innovatory aspects of VR and underestimated the human capacity to adapt to the developments of our own making.

The corporate delegates to Virtual Reality '91 hoped that VR would be ubiquituous by the end of the decade. In the meantime, however, the commercial development of virtual reality has gone largely on hold while technicians struggle to make headsets that are guaranteed not to make the user feel nauseous. While VR makes some people feel sick just by being in it, there can be no grounds for saying that we are losing the ability to tell the difference between virtual reality and real life.

For the *Sunday Times* magazine, Simon Worrall reported that

> the 'virtual' world does not yet have – and probably never will have – anything like the density and sensual immediacy of the real world. The texture of the electronic world looks like woven linen or a 3D version of one of Roy Lichtenstein's paintings. VR, like the theatre, will go on requiring the willing suspension of disbelief for some time yet.[8]

In *The Independent*, Nicholas Schoon likened his first VR experience to being

> in a cartoon room. Three dimensional, but definitely a cartoon – crude and simple, all cheerful colours. There is none of the subtlety of shading and fineness of detail found in the real world beyond the heavy headset I am wearing.[9]

Bruce Sterling, co-founder of cyberpunk along with William Gibson, was equally cautious. Of his first time in VR, Sterling reported that 'the resolution was equivalent to a cheap TV set, rather grainy and full of scan-lines; certainly there was no possibility of mistaking this for an actual "reality", or even a TV picture of an actual environment. Yet.' Cheekily, he said it was possibly more interesting to watch other people stumbling about in VR than to get in there yourself:

> The entire computer-space was also duplicated on a large TV screen, so there was no lack of amused advice from onlookers. Actually, looking on is in many ways more intriguing than being hooked up, as you watch a blindfolded person, helpless and on their back, clawing slowly at the air as if mesmerised or doing Tai Ch Ch'uan, and making occasional comments strongly reminiscent of hallucination.

'I can't grab the blue cube – help! I'm stuck behind the checkered sun!'. It's quite creepy, and has something of a bondage sado-masochism vibe.[10]

Jokingly, Sterling suggested it was possible to get off on the still-primitive character of VR and our clumsiness in using it. He too was adamant that at current levels of development, no one could mistake VR for RL. No doubt VR has become more lifelike since 1990 when Sterling wrote this piece; and no doubt it will continue to develop, albeit gradually. But even if the quality of VR imaging were to improve dramatically overnight, this does not mean that we are destined to be bamboozled by it for ever.

History is full of instances in which people have been wrong-footed initially by new technology, and then quickly learnt how to handle it. For example, the first cinema audiences in turn-of-the-century Paris mistook the train filmed by the Lumière brothers for the real thing – and they ducked under their seats in an attempt to stop it running over them. — this

But they soon learnt to distinguish between moving pictures and real life. Likewise, it is possible that the responses in Kreuger's 'duck test' will change, as soon as people become more familiar with VR.

Dr John Waldern, managing director of W Industries, the Leicester-based VR equipment manufacturers, once boasted that 'you will have to be very tough and very educated not to be enveloped in the system'.[11] But human beings are tough, especially when it comes to adapting to new experiences and learning to make sense of them. Moreover, the under-40s in the West – the people most likely to have direct experience of VR in the near future – also happen to be the most media-literate the world has ever seen. It hardly seems plausible that a generation which can spot all the cultural references in a Quentin Tarantino film will be unable to differentiate between real life and being in a 3-D version of a Roy Lichtenstein cartoon.

The school of thought which describes VR as the harbinger of a whole new era seems to have set the alarm bells ringing unnecessarily. But there is another line of thinking which holds that virtual reality has always been with us in one form or another. Predictably enough, the proponents of this strand of opinion tend to be less excitable than the 'epochal' school.

Shortly after Dr William Bricken had explained the unique effects of VR to the delegates at Virtual Reality '91, Florian Brody, of the Austrian National Library and The Voyager Co of Santa Monica, presented a paper in which he asked 'How Virtual is Reality?'[12] Brody replied that European reality, with its 'hundreds of years of cultural development', is more virtual than American reality. In particular, he cited gothic churches, *trompe l'oeil* architecture and the introduction of elaborate theatre machinery in the seventeenth century as direct precedents for current developments in VR.

With his tongue firmly in his cheek, Bruce Sterling cited the 'Sensorama Simulator' (SS) patented in 1961 by Morton L. Heilig, as a precursor of VR. The SS, according to Sterling, was 'a mechanically souped-up theatre seat involving film loops, odour canisters, and vibration. No computers, though...'[13]

Sterling was slightly more serious about the 'panorama' invented in 1785 by one Robert Barker, an Irish painter. The panorama, he explained, was

a 360-degree painted environment which used tricks of shade, lighting and stage design to present the illusion of viewer presence within a simulated realm. Some of these cunning perspective paintings were 15 metres high, 100 metres long, weighing well over 6000 kilogrammes. They were housed in huge, specially designed rotundas in London, Paris, Munich, Hamburg, Cologne, Leipzig, The Hague and many other cities.[14]

Scott Fisher, who in the second half of the eighties was founder and director of the Virtual Environment Work Station Project at Nasa's research centre near San Francisco, where he helped develop the first ever VR headset, holds that virtual reality has been in the pipeline for 30 years. Fisher also told Simon Worrall of the *Sunday Times* magazine that the desire to create and enter into simulated worlds is as old as humanity: 'The caves of Lascaux were a primitive virtual environment. The idea's been around for a long time. It's a kind of dreamspace...where you're not bound by normal laws.'[15] John Perry Barlow endorsed this view when he introduced the possibility that 'virtual reality is just another expression of what may be the third oldest human urge, the desire to have visions. Maybe we want to get high.'[16]

It seems reasonable to suppose that VR is the latest phase in a long-established tradition of simulation and stimulation – a tradition which is part of the broader tradition of humanity mediating its own experience. But if there is nothing intrinsically new about creating simulations and stimulating ourselves by entering into them, there is something fairly new about the expectation that this process irrevocably erases the distinction between fiction and fact, perception and reality. The construction of elaborate theatre machinery in the seventeenth century, for example, may have been designed to facilitate the willing suspension of disbelief. But at the time, it was understood that 'disbelief' would only be 'suspended' – in other words, it would fall into temporary disuse until the time came for *belief* to be suspended at the end of the theatrical performance. The expectation that rational individuals will be increasingly unable to maintain the fact/fiction distinction is specific to the postwar period. (In the prewar period those in authority tended to presume that the working classes would not be able to maintain the fact/fiction distinction, but this was based on the prior assumption that working-class people were not rational beings in the first place.)

During the last half-century the notion that even rational individuals might succumb to fictional worlds has been attached to successive communications technologies, including film and television. The fact that essentially the same expectation has been transferred from one technology to another suggests that this expectation is not in fact derived from any of the various technologies to which it has become attached; rather that successive technologies have at different instances become the screen upon which humanity's doubts about itself are projected.

The years since 1945 have been characterized by growing self-doubt. After the experience of economic depression and fascism in the thirties, followed by the carnage of the Second World War, the competing Big Ideas (bourgeois progress and working-class revolution) which had dominated the first half of the century were called into question. Instead of logging on to a worldview shared by millions of other people throughout society, some individuals responded to the failure of Big Ideas by experimenting with the notion of living as much as possible inside the realm of their own perceptions. Perhaps the most extreme of these responses was the formulation arrived at by the Existentialists in Paris, in which anything other than my perception of myself at the present moment, was regarded as 'bad faith'.

Anxious to avoid the allegedly totalitarian consequences of totalizing worldviews, those whom the Beat poet Allen Ginsberg described as the 'the best minds of my generation' declared that my perception is my reality, and then set out to explore the inner world of perception with the aid of hallucinogenic drugs; hence their description of themselves as 'cosmonauts of inner space'. Forty years later, their successors have hit upon cyberspace as the new form of inner space; hence the new tag, 'cybernaut'. As Sheila Johnston pointed out in *The Independent*, the conversion of LSD-guru Timothy Leary to VR ('electronic LSD') is entirely in keeping with the counterculture's heavy emphasis on personal perception. 'After all', said Johnston, 'it is a small conceptual leap from "Turn on, tune in, drop out" to "We're all living in our own Virtual Reality".'[17]

But mavericks like Leary are by no means the only ones to have made this conceptual leap. Under the rubric of social constructionism, there is now a widespread assumption to the effect that society is merely a set of shifting conventions which exists to prevent us from being entirely isolated in the virtual reality of our own perceptions. Thus, according to Sherman and Judkins 'reality is what we believe to be real'; moreover, 'virtual reality is just another reality'.[18] If the cyber-realm, as envisaged by William Gibson, is a 'consensual hallucination', this is because, according to the non-essentialist viewpoint which is dominant today, the society which gave rise to cyberspace is also a hallucination to which everyone has consented.

In those areas which are biased towards the exploration of individual perceptions, this outlook was largely welcomed. In art and music it has been the orthodox view since the fifties.

But in arenas where there was still an expectation of tangible, objectively verifiable results, the welcome was far from unequivocal. Since the publication in 1962 of *The Image*,[19] Daniel J. Boorstin's book about the suspension of reality in favour of image-making, there has been a recurring nightmare about the emergence of what is now dubbed 'virtual politics'. In *War of the Worlds*, Mark Slouka recognised the longevity of such concerns and was careful to described VR as the *final* nail in the coffin of reality.

In recent years, however, our expectations of the political realm have diminished dramatically. Politicians are no longer under any real pressure to get results. Not only do we have a new generation in power which was reared on the solipsism of the counterculture, we are also witnessing what might be described as the 'counterculturalization' of politics, whereby the countercultural notion that perception is everything has leaked into realms such as politics where objective verification has previously been an essential requirement.

In this context, Slouka and others are right to be concerned about the emergence of a new politics in which image is everything. But he is surely wrong to suggest that the technology of VR is playing the key role in bringing this about. After all, we know that communications technologies such as print (bourgeois revolutions), the telephone (the Russian Revolution), and television and the Internet (the 'velvet revolution') have always been mere instruments in the hands of political parties and their respective ideologies; and in another context, the popular expectation of VR might be, not to diminish the active self, but, in the words of a Seattle-based VR executive, 'to extend the power of the person'.[20] Far better, therefore, to try to locate the intangible and debilitating character of today's 'virtual politics' as primarily a problem of politics and ideology.

The notion of 'virtual politics' starts with the perception that we are entering into a frictionless world where we cannot get a grip on objective reality. But this is more than perception; it is itself a reality derived not from technology but from the poverty of ideas and the exhaustion of politics.

Let me illustrate my argument with a snapshot from my previous career as a left-wing news reporter. In the early nineties, I attended various demonstrations and rallies which occurred during the course of a long and controversial strike by ambulance workers. At these events, I was struck by two phenomena which I had not seen before. Firstly, the number of strikers who brought their own camcorders along in order to videotape the event. Did they expect to use such footage as an alternative source of news? No. Were they so naive that they thought going on strike was like being on holiday? Not at all. As far as I could make out, they were videoing their own strike in order to authenticate and validate it somehow; and this novel form of validation was necessitated by the fact that the organized labour movement (what was left of it) no longer had enough social weight or ideological coherence to provide a sufficient stamp of approval.

The same kind of motivation accounted for the other new phenomenon which I observed at the time – namely the presence on rally platforms of various actors who were widely known for playing the part of firefighters, ambulance drivers or hospital workers on TV. They always got the biggest round of applause – more than either union leaders or Labour and Liberal Democrat politicians. Was this because the strikers were couch potatoes who sat enthralled every night in front of their TV sets? Not at all. The loud applause for these actors was surely in tune with the fact that most people now derive a greater sense of community from the common activity of watching television than they do from their inactive membership of unions or passive support for political parties.

The media may not offer much of a sense of community; but the labour movement provided even less. And in this context it seemed to me that the applause for TV actors was a flawed attempt to reach, through them, all the other people who watch them in the same TV programmes. The strikers were by no means starstruck; but the presence of TV actors meant more to them because the mediation of experience through television was closer to their real lives than the representatives of an already outdated form of politics. In this instance, it was the labour movement that was really virtual, and the strikers responded accordingly.

The perception that our lives are somehow not being verified is by no means unique to ambulance workers. Every section of society today is immobilized, not by new media, but by the same sort of ideological impasse as that which affected the strikers of the early nineties. On the one hand, the assumption that there is no alternative to the market has never been more totalizing: the whole world accepts it. On the other hand, with few exceptions, there is no enthusiasm for the ideology of the free market. There is no apparent means of moving forward, and, as a result of this impasse, 'progress' has itself become something of a dirty word.

At a time like this when there is little sign of a convincing worldview, there is a tendency for us to take refuge in the hollow world of our own, unverified perceptions. It is this narrow frame of mind (derived from real experience), rather than the the yet-to-be experienced technology of sophisticated VR, which provides the basis for the widespread concern that we may lose the ability to get a grip. Fortunately, the pressures of economic reality are always there to stop us becoming too 'virtual'.

War/peace

The digital age has transformed war and brings new possibilities for peace. Does it really?

At Virtual Reality '94 in London, Lt Colonel Martin R. Stytz presented 'an overview of current virtual reality research and development projects by the United States Department of Defense'. Stytz cited the following projects:

> Synthetic theatre of war... its goal is to integrate live, constructive (traditional computer-based war games) and virtual environment based simulations at geographically separate sites via high-speed networks in support of joint service training exercises, doctrine development requirements, design and prototype validation and planning. The long-term goal is to bring about seamless integration of manned and semi-autonomous (unmanned, yet intelligently behaving, goal-driven) forces...
>
> Defense simulation Internet... developed as a worldwide integrated wideband network to support the real-time distributed simulation of a battle environment involving up to 100 000 entities...
>
> Air Force Institute of Technology research... broadly directed toward the investigation of the human factors, computer graphics, and human–computer interaction issues associated with the use of large-scale, distributed synthetic environments...
>
> The Synthetic BattleBridge... primary goal is to develop a system that will provide the commander with a broad range of experience in battle situations than can be gained through traditional training techniques...
>
> The Satellite Modeler... a virtual environment application that allows analyst-users to enter a virtual environment that emulates the near-Earth space environment and visualizes satellite models in their correct orbits around the Earth...
>
> The Virtual Cockpit... a low-cost flight simulator for use in a distributed interactive situation...
>
> Naval Postgraduate School Graphics and Video Laboratory

has as its research aim the development of low-cost simulators for networked virtual environment based simulations...

LORAL Advanced Distributed Simulation...has designed and developed full-crew simulators... They have also developed command post simulators...and fielded a family of semi-automated forces that emulate the behavior of friendly or enemy forces...

The University of Michigan SOAR project...providing an improved air-to-air simulated forces capability...

US Army Research Institute investigates both the behavioral science and computer science aspects of virtual environments...The broad research goal is to determine the factors that need to be addressed in order to accurately represent dismounted infantry within a virtual environment.

Stytz concluded that 'these projects have achieved some level of success in inserting manned and semi-autonomous forces into virtual battlespaces'.[1] Others, including some members of the US military, have drawn conclusions which are far more wide-ranging.

In 1994 the office of the US chief of staff sent out a press pack which announced that:

the Industrial Age is being superseded by the Information Age, the Third Wave, hard on the heels of the agrarian and industrial eras. Our present army is well-configured to fight and win in the late Industrial Age, and we can handle Agrarian-Age foes as well. We have begun to move into Third Wave warfare, to evolve a new force for a century.[2]

It sounded very much as if the chief of staff had been listening to Alvin and Heidi Toffler, the husband and wife team of futurologists whose fan base also includes senior Republican Newt Gingrich. The Tofflers originated the term 'Third Wave' in their eponymous book about the new knowledge-based economy; and in 1993 they published another book, *War and Anti-War*, in which they called for peacemaking to keep pace with the transformation of war in the Information Age:

Yet many of our intellectual weapons for peacemaking are hopelessly out of date – as are many armies. The difference is that armies all over the world are racing to meet the realities of the twenty-first century. Peacemaking, by contrast, plods along, trying to apply methods more appropriate to a distant past.[3]

Just as Marshall McLuhan had labelled the American Civil War and the First World War as 'railway wars', and described the Second World War as 'a radio war as much as it was an industrial war', so the Tofflers argued that information technology now dominates the fields of war and its prevention.

In *Wired* magazine, James Der Derian was equally convinced that ground-breaking changes had already occurred in the conduct of war. After attending a US army exercise which combined field manoeuvres with VR simulation, he suggested that 'the closer the war game was able to technically reproduce the reality of war, the greater the danger of confusing one for the other...The simulated battlefield makes dying and killing less plausible, and therefore more possible.'[4]

In the *New Statesman and Society*, Kevin Robins and Les Levidow were just as apprehensive. Noting that 'combat is increasingly mediated through the computer screen', they surmised that 'combatants are involved in a kind of remote, exhilarating tele-action, in a war sanitised of its bloody reality'. This highly mediated murder would render the victim 'psychologically invisible' to the soldier, and rob the soldier of a moral role: 'the soldier appears to a achieve a moral dissociation; the targeted "things" on the screen do not seem to implicate him in a moral relationship'.[5]

The general public, on the other hand, might become embroiled in the 'logic of fear, paranoia and aggression' as a result of watching war in the style of a video game on TV. Robins and Levidow wrote that network TV coverage of Operation Desert Storm made us 'home viewers of the Nintendo war'; we 'seemed to take pleasure in [its] viewing', and therefore remained impervious to the fate of the people in Iraq.

Robins has criticized the French postmodernist Jean Baudrillard for saying that 'the Gulf War never happened'.[6] But in so far as Baudrillard was really saying that the Gulf War was waged through images and simulation, Robins seems to be in partial argeement with him; while taking strong exception to Baudrillard's apparently cavalier attitude to the half-million Iraqi casualties of this image-making process.

Is there any truth in the suggestion that war is now a contest of information – a photo-opportunity, first and foremost? And to what extent does the deployment of new technology alter the behaviour of combatants and affect attitudes among the peoples on whose behalf they are, ostensibly, fighting?

When UN troops landed in Somalia in 1993, signalling the start of Operation Restore Hope, it seemed to the journalists in attendance that they themselves were central to what happened on the beach that day. It was as if the whole operation had been laid on for the press and broadcasting media, and some reporters came away with the impression that international relations were now subject to the newsgathering requirements of global TV stations and national newspapers. Not that these journalists were proud of their newly elevated role in the conduct of world affairs; most of them were acutely embarrassed about it. But they need not have been embarrassed, because they, and many of the theorists of the Information Age, have overestimated the part they play on the world stage.

It is certainly the case that Operation Restore Hope and Operation Desert Storm were performed with particular audiences in mind. On each occasion the USA came in search of a public theatre in which to demonstrate its leadership of the international community in front of other major powers which might have been beginning to doubt whether Uncle Sam was as unassailable and indispensable as before; and in each instance various Western governments used their participation in UN operations to showcase their moral worth in front of their own domestic populations. The fate of people in the Middle East or North Africa was never the issue of paramount concern.

Sending the right message was the priority task in both of these military operations; but this does not mean that the message-sending capacity of global media somehow provoked them or determined their outcome. Operation Desert

Storm and Operation Restore Hope entered onto the world stage through the media. But they were prompted by concerns arising from the sphere of power relations, and they were intended to influence the future conduct of power relations, either by confirming the international status of the USA or by endorsing the claims to moral authority on the part of various Western governments. In these contexts, the media can only be said to have played a mediating role in the conduct of international relations and class relations. The Information Age did not determine either the origin or the outcome of these events.

It seems that the novel character of contemporary military operations may have been exaggerated. However, this does not mean that nothing has changed: despite the protestations of time-warped leftists, the Gulf War was not fought for oil, of which there was a glut at the time; nor was it an old-style colonial war, waged in order to establish a local sphere of influence. It was, however, prompted not by the presence of the Information Age but by the absence of the Cold War and the attendant anti-communism which for 40 years had served as the rationale for American hegemony. The Gulf War was the Americans' response to their own fear that they might not be able to hold sway over the new world order; yet the readiness with which all the other Western powers lined up behind the USA suggests an unprecedented conjuncture in which the most advanced capitalist countries are more interdependent economically, and therefore more cooperative politically and militarily – at least for the time being. Moreover, they are all virtually immobilized by a sense of self-doubt. In short, geopolitical interests and ideological concerns were the decisive factors in the motivation for the Gulf War and in its conduct. The deployment of Information Age technology was purely incidental.

Equally questionable are the supposedly novel effects of digitized warfare on the soldiers who are called upon to wage it. Simulated battles are not new; they are as old as toy soldiers. Distance between combatants is nothing new either. Furthermore, wartime jargon has always been full of sporting metaphors, long before the advent of video games; and if a military man wearing a VR headset qualifies as a 'cyborg', then so does a grunt with a gun and a radio.

Desert Storm commander-in-chief General Norman Schwarzkopf liked to describe himself as a traditional 'mud soldier'. Given his key involvement in the first military exercises to incorporate computer simulations, this comment was widely thought to be disingenuous. But with hindsight it seems that Schwarzkopf was right to stress the continuities in the conduct of war, rather than get carried away with the idea that it is now a whole new ball game.

Neither is the effect of the Gulf War on the general public explicable solely in terms of the technological form in which it was presented to us. Our intake of images of war was far from unprecedented. As McLuhan observed, it was the Vietnam War which brought moving pictures of combat into America's living rooms. Moreover, if it is really the case that many of us now relate to war and the coverage of it as if we were watching it on film or as part of a videogame, this requires a political explanation rather than a technical one.

Without a thriving political arena where one might expect to exert collective pressure, everything in public life, up to and including war, tends to be experienced as something like a dream in which you cannot act or effect change even if you wanted to. Unlike the Falklands War a decade earlier, the Gulf War did not prompt outbreaks of patriotism; meanwhile opposition to the war was confined to a tiny minority. For many young people, the whole experience was bemusing. They felt uncomfortable about watching so much of it on TV; but could see no sign of a political outlook which might have brought them into the ideological fray. Thus the exhaustion of politics turns out to have been more influential than IT in formulating our conceptions of the Gulf War.

In 'peacemaking' as in warfare, the element of continuity has been underestimated. When the Tofflers call upon 'politicians and even warriors themselves' to apply 'military, economic and informational power to reduce the violence so often associated with change on the world stage', they go on to suggest that the Information Age presents new opportunities for 'action by the world community. Not crash-brigade, after-the-fact intervention but future conscious preventive action based on an understanding of the shape that the wars of tomorrow may assume.'[7] But 'future conscious preventive action' has always been the aim of the

Foreign Office and its equivalents in other Western countries. It was formerly known as 'realpolitik' and treated with due scepticism by historians and commentators. Now, apparently, the reformulation of containment and control over great swathes of the Third World can be relabelled 'anti-war' and presented as a service to humanity. The key development here is not the advance of IT but the change for the worse in the level of social criticism and historical thinking.

Likewise, in *Wired* magazine James Der Derian anticipated that the awesome capacity for information processing developed by the US Department of Defense, and the terrible reputation of 'cyber-deterrence', would lead to a situation where future conflicts might be brought to a close without a shot being fired. In fact this scenario is far from new; it is reminiscent of what used to be known as 'gunboat diplomacy', whereby major naval powers were wont to intervene in local tensions and international rivalries by despatching a heavily-gunned warship to troublesome areas. Then, as now, the message was clear – a message which has little to do with the Information Age and almost everything to do with the domination of the Third World by the competing powers of the West.

X-rated/infantilized

Self-regulation on the Internet is said to leave plenty of room for adult behaviour. Yet society now expects adults to behave more like children.

'Is the Web all sex?', asked Louise McElvogue in *The Guardian* Online.[1] She reported that 'an April [1996] survey by Nielsen Media Research showed that the online version of *Penthouse* magazine is called up thousands of times a month by employees at IBM, Apple Computer, AT&T, Nasa and Hewlett Packard'.[2] Likewise, the list of most visited sites which McElvogue obtained from another research group, Web 21, indicated that 'Playboy and a site called Sordid are up there with Time Warner's Pathfinder site and Turner's CNN'. Web 21 spokesperson Murray Bent estimated that 'about 15 per cent of traffic on the Web is to adult sites'.[3]

A year earlier, a study entitled 'Marketing Pornography on the Information Superhighway' conducted by a research team from Carnegie Mellon University, Pittsburgh, showed that trading in sexually explicit imagery is 'one of the largest (if not the largest) recreational applications of users of computer networks'.[4]

It would seem that the Internet is well stocked with 'adult' entertainment. Moreover, the failure of the old-fashioned Communications Decency Act (CDA), which sought to expunge all 'lewd, lascivious and obscene' material online but was itself expunged by the US Supreme Court as an 'unconstitutional' curb on free speech, is widely interpreted as a sign of the emergence in cyberspace of a more mature mode of control which will protect children from predatory sex-criminals while leaving adults the option to derive sexual pleasure from the content of legal Internet sites.

Thus, shortly after New Labour came to power, Home Office minister Mike O'Brien declared his support for Britain's voluntary rating and reporting agency, the Internet Watch Foundation (IWF). O'Brien promised that the government 'will work with the industry to help facilitate contacts with the police, the National Criminal Intelligence Service and international partners so that this venture can give the protection society demands for its children'.[5] Meanwhile IWF Chief Executive David Kerr sought to reassure cybercitizens that 'coded description of the content' of Internet sites, i.e. rating, would not undermine their status as autonomous adults:

> With such a label in place, anyone can use filtering software to set parameters which specify which content areas they will accept and which they reject. This approach allows both free speech to the authors on what they say, or show, and freedom of choice to users in selecting what they wish to see.[6]

IWF chairman Clive Feather, on secondment from the Internet service provider (ISP) Demon, remarked that, within the limits of the law, 'the assumption is that adults are adults, and don't need to be protected'.[7]

Among cyberculturists, the CDA is usually discounted as the final outburst of a centralised state bureaucracy which was both indiscriminate and inefficient. For the Electronic Frontier Foundation, Mike Godwin endorsed the comment made by Jonah Seiger of the Center for Democracy and Technology: 'Not only did the Court strike down the specific language of the CDA, it closed the door on future efforts to impose broadcast-style content regulations on the Internet.'[8]

While traditional, gatekeeping censorship is generally seen as a thing of the past, new regulatory institutions such as the IWF (internet watch. org. uk) tend to be judged on their ability to take account of social diffusion, individuation and the ensuing proliferation of different codes and standards. At a forum on censorship sponsored by the Internet Developers' Association, John Browning, (then) executive editor of *Wired* (UK), stressed the distinction between 'a censor rather than *the* censor – the difference is crucial'.[9] At the same event, the Internet's first British millionaire Peter Dawe launched what was to become the IWF (initially it was known as the Safety Net Foundation) with the promise that his initiative would provide 'multiple censors – you choose your own censor'.[10]

A fortnight later, alongside the London Internet Exchange (Linx) and the executive committee of the Internet Service

Providers' Association (UK), the IWF/Safety Net Foundation recommended 'an industry proposal' for 'rating, reporting, responsibility' [R3] with regard to 'child pornography and illegal material on the Internet'. Its proponents were keen to stress that this was not censorship in the traditional sense. Instead they explained that adult 'consumers should have the technological means to tailor their, or their family's experience on the Internet according to their individual standards; thus supporting both individual responsibility and the Internet's traditions of diversity and free speech'.[11]

Likewise, at the high-profile press launch of the 'R3' document, Ian Taylor, Minister for Science and Technology in John Major's Conservative government, emphasized that:

> this is not a question of censoring legal material or free speech... The core of this initiative is about dealing with material which breaks our existing laws, particularly where child pornography is involved. It is also about consumers as parents and teachers being able to control the Net access of the young and vulnerable in their charge, according to their own individual standards.[12]

Business Week magazine had already called for governments to step back and 'let parents do the policing'.[13] In 1995, Microsoft and Netscape suspended hostilities (temporarily) and set up the Information Highway Parental Empowerment Group which aimed to 'help parents protect their children from electronic porn'. The *Financial Times* reported that the Trove Investment Corporation of Vancouver had launched Net Nanny, 'a $49 software package for the Windows or DOS environment' which would allow parents to block their children's access to whatever they (the parents) considered 'inappropriate material'.[14] In July 1996, the UK subsidiary of the American ISP Netcom launched a national advice service with the avowed intention of giving 'parents enough information to empower them to select and regulate a child's usage of the Internet'.[15]

In July 1997, Kerr of the IWF insisted that his proposals to the Global Information Networks conference in Bonn would 'let parents customise exactly what their children can and cannot see'.[16] The Cambridge-based company which developed Guardian Agent, perhaps the most sophisticated blocking software to date, goes by the name of Autonomy; thereby echoing the widespread assumption that this kind of technology and the accompanying debate can only increase the empowerment of parents and confirm their status as autonomous adults.

This is plausible, technically. It is not hard to envisage a situation in which the application of such technology would have exactly that effect. But we are living in a completely different context, where parents are already under intense scrutiny of an entirely negative kind. After centuries of being 'natural' and unproblematic, bringing up children (aka 'parenting') now prompts heated arguments, hysterical reactions and wholesale intervention by a proliferation of semi-official agencies.

In this climate, parents are under increasing pressure to demonstrate their sense of responsibility towards their offspring, otherwise it may be assumed that they have been irresponsible or even abusive in their dealings with them. Failure to follow recommended ratings (even if these are entirely inappropriate for the individual children concerned) is tantamount to 'parental neglect'.

The emergence of the IWF and the development of blocking software seem to exemplify what David Lyon of Queen's University has dubbed 'sociality' – self-regulation on the part of individuals in the absence of centralized agencies of control. At a conference on the 'governance of cyberspace' at the University of Teesside in April 1995, Lyon expounded on the concept of 'sociality' as a progressive approach to social control:

> The concept of sociality offers one such new direction. Here the focus turns to responsible action rather than regulation and compliance. Social reality is a dialectic of the playful and the patterned; authority is plural and choice is central. Linked with an ontology and an ethic of the Other who has claims upon us, new approaches may be available for the most pressing problems of cyberspace and surveillance.[17]

But who is to say what constitutes 'responsible action'? In the case of children and the Internet, will it really be parents who make their own choices, according to their intimate experience of their own children? Or is it more likely that parents will be pressured into making 'informed choices', that is, choices informed by advice from agencies such as the British Board of Film Classification, which is already involved in issuing such advice in respect of videos and computer games? If events take the latter course, then the 'concept of sociality' turns out to be not so new after all. It transpires that 'sociality' is in fact a magnification of the 'inner policeman' identified by Trotsky as the internalized law-enforcer who is spontaneously generated in capitalist society.

The journalist and privacy activist Simon Davies recognizes the element of coercion underneath the jargon of empowerment and free choice. At a seminar on Civil Liberties and the Internet held at King's College, London, Davies pointed out that 'what is portrayed as voluntary' is often 'an incursion on the individual rights' of adults.[18] While ostensibly endorsing our rights and confirming the distinction between adults and children, the pressure on parents to adhere to the 'voluntary' advice dished out by a whole host of new institutions is really as degrading as the directly coercive forms of censorship used against the masses by the old-fashioned state. The latter were a straightforward assault on individual autonomy, while the former has the effect of eroding adulthood, thereby bringing parents down towards the same social level as their children.

If Internet users are under 'voluntary' pressure to dumb down, so are the industry's content providers. After a 'censorware summit' at the White House in July 1997, President Bill Clinton concluded that 'we need to encourage every Internet site, whether or not it has material harmful to minors, to rate its contents'.[19] Major players on the Internet are currently pressurizing each other to fall in line with Clinton's message. Robert Davis, president of Lycos, the 3W search engine, told Declan McCullagh of the *Netly News* that during the meeting with Clinton: 'I threw a gauntlet to other search engines that collectively we should require a rating before we index pages.'[20]

Likewise, the British 'industry proposal' endorsed by successive Tory and New Labour governments, recommended that ISPs 'require all their users to rate their own web pages using RSACi' (the rating scheme drawn up by the US Recreational Software Advisory Committee), and urged ISPs to 'remove web pages hosted on their servers which are persistently and deliberately misrated'.[21] The proposal contained similar policies with respect to Usenet news groups. In every corner of cyberspace, pressure to 'self-label' is mounting.

Voluntary rating may seem unproblematic; except that, as we have seen, while not compulsory by law it is not voluntary either. Moreover, the requirement that the content of online communication should be set and classified in advance is itself inimical to the mobility and flexibility previously associated with adulthood.

The Roman comic playwright Terence put the following line into the mouth of one his characters: 'Homo sum; humani nil a me alienum puto' ['I am a man; I hold that nothing human is alien to me']. This line connotes a selfhood which can cope with the full range of human behaviour and the transition from one behavioural facet to another; a sense of self, therefore, which is commensurate with the concept of the autonomous legal subject.

In today's society, however, the fluid notion of the legal subject who is capable and therefore culpable, is gradually being replaced by a static sense of self as cultural personality. Selfhood is increasingly couched in terms of personal taste. Personal growth consists of expanding one's experiential range by visiting new locations, the content of which will have been prescribed in advance. In this way, the (non-) adult self is sheltered like a minor from the unpredictability of unmoderated interaction. Likewise, calls for the advance rating of all online material suggest a diminished range of interaction more suited to children who need sheltering than to adults who have traditionally defined themselves as such by their ability to cope with the unrestrained dynamism of human society.

The idea of choosing a censor according to personal taste is also an expression of infantilization. Writing in the *Daily Telegraph* a few weeks after the launch of the Internet Watch Foundation, *Wired* editor John Browning welcomed the fact that 'the technology of the Internet can provide every community with the ability to censor whatever it might find offensive',[22] thereby removing from government the undesirable role of censoring offensive material on behalf of various different constituencies. Again, Browning's observation sounds unexceptionable at first. But on closer inspection, it is found to contain an idea of communities realizing themselves as such by identifying what they find offensive and taking steps to ensure that they never have to look it in the face. The inability to cope, the refusal to look reality in the face: these are characteristics of the child rather than the adult; and in this respect the D-I-Y censorship recommended first by Dawe and then by Browning is characteristic of an infantilized sense of self which is antithetical to adult autonomy.

Chris Ellison of the Internet Freedom Campaign (net freedom. org) has pointed out that the primary case against pornography, namely that it prompts individuals to imitate in real life what they have seen depicted on screen, also assumes that these same individuals are childlike and immature rather than adult and rational. Furthermore, the overall effect of successive panics about computer pornography and vulnerable children is to reconfigure society's mental picture of the Internet so that it comes to be dominated by a fairy tale idea of how children are affected by what they may or may not have seen online. Again, the child's eye view – or, rather, a perception of the child's eye view – takes precedence over all other considerations. Meanwhile, at the other end of the spectrum, the apparent preoccupation with sex on the part of many Internet users also seems to reflect a somewhat childish, behind-the-bike-sheds view of what it means to be adult. Among the consumers of erotica and its opponents, the child's eye view seems to be the dominant outlook of the day.

Thus both the presence of 'adult' material on the Internet and the ostensible attempts to deal with it 'as adults' are in fact expressions of the current trend for adults to identify themselves with children and the childlike. Online and off, X-rated material offers no protection against the insidious process of infantilization.

Youth/age

In cyberculture no one is middle-aged, which means that no one can be young either.

Cyberculture is full of what marketing men now refer to as 'Middle Youth'. In *The Independent*, media correspondent Paul McCann defined Middle Youth as:

> a new kind of consumer, greying groovers who refuse to grow old gracefully; people from their late twenties to their early forties who cling to the trappings of youth. These are people with a concern about fashion, a wild social life and an up-to-date record collection, but who are at the same time old enough to have a nice house, a garden, children and responsibilities. They exist thanks to better careers for women, couples having children much later in life and the fact that 'youth culture' and all its trappings is the dominant cultural form of the Nineties.[1]

Whereas middle age is traditionally associated with substance, stability and the long term, cyberculture celebrates instantaneity, fluidity and the use of illicit substances. But these preoccupations are no longer the preserve of youth. Online and off, the people who share these priorities could be 14 or 45. The Generation Gap has been closing for some time now; and in the new terrain of cyberspace it has never really existed.

This poses a problem for young people. How, in such a context, can they differentiate themselves from their elders? They may want to rebel, but the rebel stance is still monopolized by their parents. It seems that youth is being denied its birthright by an older generation that refuses to grow up. In fact 'youth culture' never belonged to young people in the first place; it has always been an exaggerated expression of what was already going on in the minds of their elders.

For example, in the seminal James Dean film *Rebel Without a Cause*, the character of Jim Stark is defined by his lack of self-definition. He is unable to do what he thinks is expected of him, and uncertain of what else to do. In the mythology of 'youth culture', Dean/Stark is suffering from the effects of old-style parental discipline. But in Nicholas Ray's film his father is not at all the patriarch. In one scene he is seen wearing a pinafore, and when Dean/Stark demands some answers, far from replying in a stentorian tone of voice, his father is unable to say anything decisive. In short, the uncertainty of the parents is writ large in the indecision of the son. Likewise the doubts and disengagement at the core of 'youth culture' were, even in the mid-fifties, a projection of the self-alienation which the adult world was already starting to experience.

The adult origins of 'youth culture' were first demonstrated by the American literary critic John W. Aldridge. Writing towards the end of the sixties, Aldridge bemoaned the fact that by 1970 'this country will have been dominated by children for almost twenty-five years'. But he also pointed out that his generation 'had taught them [youth] by our example';[2] rather than going against the grain of postwar society, the young and their counterculture represented, in an intensified form, the direction in which that society was already going.

In the early sixties various commentators pointed out that youth was no longer the anteroom to adulthood, full of young people queueing up to be admitted. But it was only when grown-ups stopped believing in adulthood that young people followed suit.[3] If the youth in cyberculture really want to strike out on their own, they might like to start addressing the question which their parents and grandparents have been ducking for the last 50 years: what does it mean to be an adult?

Zero sum game/everything to play for

There is currently a prejudice against progress which holds that human activity must be curtailed. But the Internet demonstrates the potential for humanity to enjoy an unlimited future history.

> In a situation where change has long ceased to be all progress, if it ever was, and where what progress is has become eminently disputable, the preservation and renewal of tradition, as well as of environmental resources, take on a particular urgency.[1]

In one of the first books to recognise the end of the long-standing left/right divide, Anthony Giddens (then a Cambridge don, latterly the director of the London School of Economics) nominated 'philosophic conservatism' as the new form of 'radical politics'. These are strange days, indeed, when probably the premier sociologist in Britain seeks to redefine radicalism according to the principles of the arch-conservative Edmund Burke.

The following year, 1995, against a background of rising panic about 'mad cow disease', Giddens addressed a conference on the 'risk society' hosted by the Institute of Contemporary Arts, London, and convened by the Institute for Public Policy Research. Speaking without notes, he gave a bravura performance which stole the show from Ulrich Beck, the other weighty academic at the event. Despite the droll delivery, however, the content of Giddens' remarks was timid in the extreme. He warned that living in a world of accelerated change and 'manufactured uncertainty' requires a greater degree of circumspection on our part:

> All of us now live at the barbaric final frontier of high technology...Manufactured uncertainty is expanding in most domains of human life...it intrudes directly into personal and social life. There is a new riskiness to risk which is largely incalculable. Just as in the case of Chernobyl, in the case of mad cow disease no one knows [how

many people will be affected]. The risk is probably very small, but you cannot know.[2]

The phrase 'you cannot know' is highly characteristic of our times. It has become something of a mantra, to be repeated whenever experimentation is called for. In previous decades, the unpredictability of results would not have been seen as a prohibitive argument against experimentation. But today's society has embraced the 'precautionary principle', which dictates that nothing should be ventured unless its outcome can be guaranteed in advance – a principle which, had it been adopted at the end of the fifteenth century, would have meant Christopher Columbus staying at home in Spain rather than risking falling off the edge of the world and thereby finding the 'new world' instead.

Giddens is perhaps the most sophisticated exponent of a new sensibility which interprets human history as a zero sum game; not as a paradigm of progress but rather as a continuum of hubris and its horrendous consequences. We have gained little or nothing, it is said, from the last two centuries of industrialization, except perhaps the all-too-recent recognition that we have gained nothing.

This fatalistic sensibility amounts to a collective loss of nerve on the part of society as a whole; and it is discernible throughout the whole of society, from the new-found preference among professional economists for measuring performance according to a 'quality of life index' rather than traditional growth indicators such as gross domestic product, to popular hostility towards the eighties – the decade associated with the free market maxim articulated by Gordon Gekko as portrayed by Michael Douglas in Oliver Stone's film *Wall Street*: 'Greed is good'.

As soon as it is accepted that the idea of progress has got us into a zero sum game, growth can only regarded as gross; greed becomes the deadliest of sins; and caution must be the only virtue which can rescue humanity from the hell we have made for ourselves. Advocating caution was until recently the chosen role of a tiny minority. The ruling elite hitherto sought to demonstrate its right to rule by reference to concepts such as dynamism, abundance and wealth. But in today's climate these are strangely unfashionable. Such is the failure of nerve among the bourgeoisie that industry is currently unable to utilize its own capacity for innovation and growth. More generally, the sense that life is a no-win situation is now a profoundly debilitating influence which may well develop into a self-fulfilling prophesy.

In this context, as we have seen, cyberspace is often talked about as the latest in a long line of places where humanity is destined to screw up. Even those who are enthusiastic about developments such as the Internet may well be reproducing this fashionable fatalism in a different form. Thus digital communications are sometimes celebrated as the post-industrial arena in which old-fashioned industrial growth is unnecessary. In this respect the preference for the 'Information Age' over the 'Industrial Age' is really another way of retreating from the same social problems and their apparent intractability.

I beg to differ. In my opinion, the biggest problem in society today is not the uncontrolled whirlwind of industry and the marketplace (would that this was the case!) but rather the culture of constraint that would finally abandon the aspirations of the Enlightenment and redefine civilization as mere survival with equity and e-mail. I prefer to envisage the information superhighway as a problem-solving tool with the potential to increase dramatically industrial production. Likewise, I strongly disagree with the notion of the Internet as an expression of de-centred nature reasserting itself over the flawed foci of human civilization. I envisage it as a mechanism which could play an important role in helping humanity to mediate the laws of nature and gain greater control over our circumstances.

Digital communications contain within them the limitless prospect of our future history; meanwhile society's expectations of cyberspace reflect the diminished stature of humanity in our own eyes. This is just one of the many contradictions which typify the peculiar intensity of our current predicament.

Notes and References

ANARCHY/AUTHORITY

1. Headline in *The Guardian*, 6 January 1995.
2. Peter Hannington, 'Anarchy on the Internet', *New Times*, 15 April 1995.
3. Professor Ian Angell, 'The Information Revolution and the Death of the Nation State', *LSE magazine*, summer 1995.
4. Robert Reich, *The Work of Nations: Preparing Ourselves for Twenty-first-Century Capitalism* (London: Simon & Schuster, 1991), p. 3.
5. Martin Jacques, 'The End of Politics', *Sunday Times*, 18 July 1993.
6. 'Parade of the Mastodons', *Wall Street Journal*, 21 July 1993.
7. 'The Vision Machine', Paul Virilio (London: British Film Institute Publications, 1994).
8. Simon Davies, 'Welcome Home, Big Brother', *Wired (UK)*, May 1995, p. 110.
9. Brent Gregston, 'Open Secrets', *Internet*, November 1995, p. 29.
10. Bill Thompson, 'Watching the Virtual Detectives', *.net*, May 1995.
11. Paul H. A. Frissen, Tilburg University, The Netherlands, 'The Virtual State: Postmodernisation, Informatisation and Public Administration', paper to the Governance of Cyberspace conference, University of Teesside, 12–13 April 1995. A version of this paper was subsequently published in *The Governance of Cyberspace*, edited by Brian Loader (London: Routledge, 1997).
12. Marshall McLuhan and Bruce Powers, The Global Village (New York: Oxford University Press 1989), p. 118.
13. Anne W. Branscomb, 'Common Law for the Electronic Frontier', *Scientific American*: the computer in the 21st century, special issue 1995, p. 160.
14. Ibid.
15. John Kay, 'Threats to Bill Gates and the Internet', *Financial Times*, 15 December 1995.
16. Simon Davies, *Big Brother: Britain's Web of Surveillance and the New Technological Order* (London: Pan, 1994).
17. Robin Cook, 'Byte-sized Revolution', *New Statesman and Society* 5 August 1994.

18. Al Gore, 'Infrastructure for the Global Village', *Scientific American*: the computer in the 21st century, special issue 1995, p. 157.
19. Jonathon Carr-Brown, 'Blair aims to "do a Kennedy" on Net', *Sunday Times*, 8 September 1997.

BOYS/GIRLS

1. Sadie Plant, 'Babes in the Net', *New Statesman and Society*, 27 February 1995.
2. Robin Hunt, 'Internet Anoraks On Line to Become Dirty Mac Brigade at Touch of Button', *The Guardian*, London, 11 July 1996.
3. 'Men, Women and Computers: The Gender Gap in High Tech', *Newsweek* cover story, 16 May 1994.
4. *Gender Wars*, reviewed in Connected, the IT supplement to the *Daily Telegraph*, 16 July 1996.
5. Victoria Griffith, 'Gender Lines Lead to a Goldmine', *Financial Times*, 1 July 1996.
6. Donna J. Haraway, 'A Cyborg Manifesto: Science, Technology and Socialist Feminism in the Late Twentieth Century', in *Simians, Cyborgs and Women: The Reinvention of Nature* (London: Free Association Books, 1991).

COMMUNITY/ALIENATION

1. Howard Rheingold, *The Virtual Community: Finding Connection in a Computerized World* (London: Secker & Warburg, 1994), pp. 1–3.
2. Cristina Odone, 'A Patchwork of Catholic Tastes', *The Guardian*, 18 September 1995, p. 10.
3. Kevin speaking at the conference on Culture, Technology and Creativity, Institute of Contemporary Arts, London, 6 April 1992.
4. John Gray, 'Cyber-utopia?' *The Guardian*, 10 April 1993.
5. Vivian Sobchack, 'Reading *Mondo 2000*', in Mark Dery (ed.), *Flame Wars: The Discourse of Cyberculture*, in *The South Atlantic Quarterly*, Fall 1993 (vol. 92, no. 4) Durham, North Carolina: Duke University Press.
6. Bruce Sterling, 'Preface', *Mirrorshades* (London: Paladin, 1988), p. ix.
7. Bill Gates cited in John Seabrook, *Deeper: A Two-Year Odyssey in Cyberspace* (London: Faber & Faber, 1997), quoted in 'Con-

versations with a Nerd', *The Observer Review*, 2 March 1997, p. 5.

8. Rheingold, *The Virtual Community* p. 3.
9. Ziauddin Sardar, 'alt.civilizations.faq: cyberspace as the darker side of the West', in *futures: the journal of forecasting, planning and policy*, special issue: cyberspace, to boldly go (Oxford: Elsevier Science Ltd), vol. 27, no. 7, September 1995, pp. 787–8.
10. Lyn Nell Hancock and Rob French, 'The Dawn of On-Line Home Schooling', *Newsweek*, 10 October 1994, p. 50.
11. Graeme Kidd, 'A Fair Cop', *Computer Shopper*, March 1994.
12. Stephen Graham, 'Flight to the Cyber-Suburbs', *The Guardian*, OnLine supplement, 18 April 1996, pp. 2–3.
13. Jim McClellan, 'Netsurfers', *The Observer*, Life supplement, 13 February 1994, pp. 8–10.
14. Gail Robinson, 'A Net Tribute', *Internet*, November 1997, pp. 60–3.
15. Tony Blair, speech to the TUC conference, Brighton, 9 September 1997.

DEMOCRACY/DIVERSITY

1. 'The Wired Manifesto for the Digital Society', by the editors of *Wired (UK)*, October 1996, pp. 42–7.
2. Jon Katz, 'The Age of Paine', Wired (UK), premiere edition, April 1995, pp. 64–9.
3. Howard Rheingold, 'Networking Brings Power to the People', *Daily Telegraph*, 15 December 1994.
4. Joshua Quittner, 'Dining with the EFF', *Wired*, San Francisco, June 1994, pp. 80–1 and pp. 128–31.
5. Ibid.
6. James Carey, 'The Mythos of the Electronic Revolution', in *Communication as Culture: Essays on Media and Society* (Winchester, Massachusetts: Unwin Hyman, 1989), quoted by Howard Rheingold in *The Virtual Community: Finding Connection in a Computerized World* (London: Secker & Warburg, 1994), p. 286.
7. Howard Rheingold, *The Virtual Community: Finding Connection in a Computerized World* (London: Secker & Warburg, 1994), p. 289.
8. Press release issued by Digital Diaspora to publicize a 'black cyberspace conference' entitled 'Forty Acres And A Micorchip' which took place in June 1995 at the National Film Theatre, London.

9. Kobena Mercer, 'Welcome to the Jungle: Identity and Diversity in Postmodern Politics', in Jonathan Rutherford (ed.), *Identity: Community, Culture, Difference* (London: Lawrence & Wishart, 1993), p. 50.
10. Kenan Malik, 'Universalism and Difference: Race and the Postmodernists', in *Race & Class*, 37(3) (1996).
11. Hippolyte Taine quoted in Kenan Malik, Universalism and Difference: Race and the Postmodernists', in *Race & Class*, 37 (3) (1996).

EQUALITY/ELITISM

1. Al Gore quoted in the Financial Times Survey of International Telecommunications, published with the *Financial Times*, 17 October 1994.
2. Felix Houphouet-Boigny quoted in Gary Stix and Paul Wallich, 'A Digital Fix for the Third World?', in *The Computer in the 21st Century*, special issue of *Scientific American*, vol. 6, no. 1, 1995, p. 43.
3. Bill Gates, *The Road Ahead* (New York: Viking, 1995), quoted in 'Virtual Capitalism: The Political Economy of the Information Highway', *Monthly Review*, vol. 48, no. 3, July–August 1996.
4. Andrew Adonis, 'It is Time to Cut through the Hype', Financial Times Survey of International Telecommunications, published with the *Financial Times*, 17 October 1994.
5. Victor Keegan, 'The Wired and the Unwired', *Times Literary Supplement*, 4 July 1997, p. 6.
6. 'Cyberspace: The New Elite', front cover feature, *Time* magazine, 4 October 1997.
7. 'The New Establishment – Leaders of the Information Age', *Vanity Fair*, October 1995, p. 141.
8. Arthur Kroker and Michael A. Weinstein, *Data Trash: The Theory of the Virtual Class* (Montreal: New World Perspectives 1994), p. 7.
9. Langdon Winner, *The Whale and the Reactor* (Chicago: University of Chicago Press, 1986), p. 112.
10. Paul Foot, *The Politics of Harold Wilson* (Harmondsworth: Penguin, 1968).

FREE/FEE

1. Andrew Orlowski, 'Absolutely No Net Profits', *The Independent*, 3 April 1995, p. 23.
2. 'The Software Industry Survey', *The Economist*, 25 May 1996, p. 4.
3. 'The Death of Distance; A Survey of Telecommunciations', *The Economist*, 30 September 1995, p. 5.
4. John Battelle quoted by Andrew Leonard, 'Hot-Wired', *The Bay Guardian*, California, cited in Arthur Kroker and Michael A. Weinstein, *Data Trash: The Theory of the Virtual Class* (Montreal: New World Perspectives, 1994), p. 4.
5. R.U. Sirius, 'A User's Guide to Using This Guide', in *Mondo 2000: A User's Guide*, (New York: Harper Books, 1992), p 16.
6. John Gray and David Willetts, *Is Conservatism Dead?* (London: Social Market Foundation, 1997).
7. Text for an advertisement for a conference on Corporate Citizenship which took place at Church House conference centre, London, on 4 November 1997. The advertisement was published in the *New Statesman*, 17 October 1997, p. 58.
8. R.U. Sirius, quoted in 'Sex, Drugs and Cyberspace', *Express: The East Bay's Free Weekly*, California, 28 September 1990, p. 12.

GATES/ANTI-GATES

1. Steven Levy, 'The Microsoft Century', *Newsweek*, 2 December 1996.
2. Walter Isaacson, 'In Search of the Real Bill Gates', *Time*, 13 January 1997.
3. Ibid.
4. Levy, *The Microsoft Century*.
5. 'Today The Internet, Tomorrow the World', *The Guardian*, Online supplement, 17 October 1996.
6. Bill Gates, *The Road Ahead*, quoted in Matt Labash, 'Gates of Hell', *Sunday Telegraph* 19 January 1997, p. 6.
7. John Seabrook, *Deeper: A Two-Year Odyssey in Cyberspace* (London: Faber & Faber, 1997).
8. John Seabrook, 'Conversations with a Nerd', *The Observer Review*, 2 March 1997, p. 5.
9. Esther Dyson quoted in Walter Isaacson, 'In Search of the Real Bill Gates', *Time*, 13 January 1997.

10. Steve Jobs in 'Triumph of the Nerds', documentary programme for Channel 4 television, 1995.
11. Labash, 'Gates of Hell', p. 6.
12. Jim McClellan, 'The Geek Factory', *The Observer*, Life magazine, 12 November 1995.
13. Douglas Coupland, *Microserfs* (London: Flamingo, 1995).
14. Bill Gates quoted in Isaacson, 'In Search of the Real Bill Gates'.
15. Edward Tenner, *Why Things Bite Back* (London: Fourth Estate, 1996).
16. Bill Gates quoted in Seabrook, 'Conversations with a Nerd', p. 5.
17. Ibid.

HACKING/SLACKING

1. Nick Rosen, 'Young Gifted and Hacking Away', Online supplement, *The Guardian*, 17 November 1994, p. 9.
2. Tim Kelsey, 'Revealed: How Hacker Penetrated the Heart of British Intelligence', *The Independent*, 24 November 1994, pp. 1–3.
3. Patrick Fitzgerald, 'BT the First Casualty in Intelligence Phoney War', *New Statesman and Society*, 2 December 1994.
4. Michelle Slatalla and Joshua Quittner, *Masters Of Deception: The Gang Who Ruled Cyberspace* (London: Vintage, 1995).
5. James Adams, 'Russian Computer Hackers Alarm FBI', *Sunday Times*, 12 February 1995.
6. John Sweeney, 'To Catch a Hacker', *Life* magazine, *The Observer*, 4 September 1994.
7. Fitzgerald, 'BT The First Casualty'.
8. Charles Platt, 'Hackers: Threat or Menace', *Wired*, November 1994, pp. 82–8.
9. Ibid.
10. Ibid.
11. Gareth Branwyn, 'Cyberpunk', in Rudy Rucker, R.U. Sirius and Queen Mu, *Mondo 2000: A User's Guide to the New Edge* (New York: Harper Books, 1992), p. 66.
12. Vivian Sobchack, 'Democratic Franchise And The Electronic Frontier', in 'Cyberspace: To Boldly Go', special edition of *futures* journal, edited by Ziauddin Sardar and Jerome R. Ravetz (Oxford: Elsevier), vol. 27, no. 7, September 1995, p. 731.
13. Ibid.
14. Nick Rosen, 'Young Gifted and Hacking Away', p. 9.

15. Emily Benedek, 'Hack to the Future', *Details*, December 1994, pp. 52–64.
16. Ibid.
17. Wendy Grossman, 'Hacking with the Enemy', Online supplement, *The Guardian*, Thursday 11 July 1996, p. 4.
18. Ibid.
19. Ibid.
20. Douglas Coupland, *Generation X* (London: Abacus, 1992).
21. Dennis Hayes, *Behind the Silicon Curtain: The Seductions of Work in a Lonely Era* (London: Free Association Books, 1989), p. 93.
22. Oliver Harris, 'Introduction' to *The Letters of William S. Burroughs* (London: Picador, 1993), p. XXIII.

INNOVATION/STAGNATION

1. David Bowen, 'The Future is Virtually Here', *The Independent on Sunday*, 15 July 1993, p. 19.
2. John May, 'The Shape of Things to Come', *Telegraph* magazine, 19 November 1994, p. 18.
3. Ibid.
4. Ibid.
5. 'Welcome to the Revolution', *Fortune* magazine, 13 December 1993.
6. Charles Handy, 'The Knowledge Economy', *Financial Times*, 29 December 1993.
7. Steven Levy, 'Technomania', in 'Technology '95 – The Future isn't What You Think', *Newsweek*, 27 February 1995, pp. 13–17.
8. Ibid.
9. James Woodhuysen, 'Before We Rush to Declare a New Era', Special issue on 'Liberation Technology?', *Demos Quarterly*, Issue 4, 1994, p. 7.
10. Woodhuysen, *op. cit.*, p. 8. His reference is to James Beniger, *The Control Revolution* (Harvard University Press, 1989).
11. Woodhuysen, *op. cit.*, p. 8.
12. Author's notes from the Culture, Technology and Creativity Conference, Institute of Contemporary Arts, April 1991.
13. Author's notes.
14. Author's notes.
15. Simson Garfinkel, 'Has Anyone Seen HAL?', *Wired (UK)*, pp. 54 and 96.
16. Woodhuysen, *op. cit.*, p. 7.

17. Mark Prendergast, 'CD-Rom Wasn't Built in a Day', *New Statesman and Society*, 24 June 1994, pp. 31–2.
18. Ibid.
19. Ibid.
20. Hari Kunzru, 'Novel Way of Seeing the Net', interview with Chris Locke, *Daily Telegraph*, Connected supplement, 9 September 1997, p. 11.
21. *The Economist*, 13 February 1993.
22. Child and Loveridge, *Information Technology in European Services* (London, 1990), p. 355.

JOURNALISM/PERSONALISM

1. Peter McGrath, 'The Daily Me', *Newsweek*, 6 June 1994, p. 27.
2. Mock-up produced by the Guardian Media Laboratories and issued free with *The Guardian* newspaper, 1 December 1994.
3. Tony Hall quoted in Andrew Culf, 'Slave New World?', *The Guardian*, Media section, Monday 13 November 1995.
4. Victoria Griffith, 'Your Newspaper is Ready Now', *Financial Times*, Media Futures page, 29 July 1996.
5. Ibid.
6. Ibid.
7. Mark Edwards, 'The Day We Got Our Names Back', *Evening Standard*, 12 October 1994, p. 59.
8. Karl Marx and Friedrich Engels, *Werke*, supplementary volume 1 (Berlin, Harausgegeben vom Institut für Marxismus-Leninismus beim ZK der SED: 1956–68), p. 405.
9. Marx and Engels, *Werke*, volumes 1, 6.
10. Stan Le Peak quoted in Victoria Griffith, 'Your Newspaper is Ready Now', *Financial Times*, Media Futures page, Monday 29 July 1996.

KNOCKERS/BOOSTERS

1. Nicholas Negroponte, *Being Digital* (London: Hodder & Stoughton, 1994).
2. Ian Hislop, 'Looking for Laughs', *The Guardian*, 20 September 1995.
3. Janet Street-Porter, 'Forget the Superhighway, Get a Life', *The Times*, 19 March 1996.

4. Toby Young, 'Is the Internet the CB Radio of the 90s?', *Vanity Fair*, October 1995.

5. Theodore Roszak, *The Making of a CounterCulture: The Technocratic Society and its Youthful Opposition* (London: Faber & Faber, 1970).

6. Theodore Roszak, *The Cult of Information: The Folklore of Computers and the True Art of Thinking* (San Francisco: Pantheon, 1986).

7. Clifford Stoll, *Silicon Snake Oil: Second Thoughts on the Information Highway* (London: Macmillan, 1995).

8. James Brook and Iain A. Boal, *Resisting the Virtual Life: The Culture and Politics of Information* (San Francisco: City Lights, 1995), Preface, p. xiv.

9. Gertrude Himmelfarb, *The Idea of Poverty: England in the Early Industrial Age* (London: Faber & Faber, 1985), p. 365.

LOGICAL/MYSTICAL

1. Steven R. Holtzman, *Digital Mantras: The Language of Abstract and Virtual Worlds* (London: The MIT Press, 1994), pp. 125–9.

2. Ibid., pp. 291–2.

3. Ibid., p. 293.

M-O-R/COUNTERCULTURE

1. George Wallace quoted in Neil Buckley, 'Slow Stroll to the Virtual Mall', *Financial Times*, 24 April 1995.

2. Louise Kehoe, 'Online for a Speedy Sale', *Financial Times*, 23 June 1994, p. 18.

3. Jim McClellan, 'Log On, Click In, Get Addicted', *The Observer* preview, 28 April–4 May 1996, pp. 6–7.

4. Ibid.

5. Andrew Brown, 'The Tedium is the Technology', *The Independent*, 28 January 1994, p. 13.

6. Tom Wolft, *The Electric Kool Aid Acid Test* (New York: Farrar, Straus & Giroux, 1968)

7. Author's notes from interview with William Gibson, parts of which were published in *G Spot* magazine (ceased publication), London, May 1994.

8. Ibid.

9. Ibid.

10. Douglas Rushkoff, *Cyberia: Life in the Trenches of Hyperspace* (London: HarperCollins, 1994), pp. 287–8.
11. Barry Diller, speech to Edinburgh TV Festival, August 1994, as issued to the press.
12. Robert Brustein, *Revolution as Theatre: Notes on the New Radical Style* (New York: Liveright, 1971).

NOSTALGIA/FUTURISM

1. Jim McClellan, 'The Man Who Made Cyberspace', *The Face*, September 1992, pp. 63–6.
2. Author's transcript of interview with William Gibson.
3. William Gibson, 'The Gernsback Continuum', in Bruce Sterling (ed.), *Mirrorshades* (London: Paladin, 1989).
4. Fraser Clark quoted in Jules Marshall, 'The Zippies', *Wired*, 1994.
5. Jules Marshall, 'The Zippies', *Wired*, 1994.
6. Michel Serres, *Angels*, (London: Flammarion, 1996).
7. Steve Mizrach, aka Seeker 1, 'Modern Primitives: The Accelerating Collision of Past and Future in the Postmodern Era', at the Cyberanthropology site, http//www.clas.ufl.edu/anthro/modern_primitive.html.
8. Ibid.
9. Mark Dery, *Escape Velocity* (London: Hodder & Stoughton, 1996).

OVERLOAD/INFORMATION

1. John Naughton, 'Trying to Track Something Down? Unleash Your Cyberhound', *The Observer Review*, 2 November 1997, p. 8.
2. Design Agenda conference, Central School of Art, London, July 1996, author's notes.
3. Victor Keegan, 'Brain Storms', tabloid section, *The Guardian*, 5 November 1996, pp. 2–3.
4. Ibid.
5. William Gibson quoted in Chris Mitchell, 'Books Byte Back', *.net*, September 1997.
6. Douglas Rushkoff quoted in Louise McElvogue, 'Zapped By The Cyberpunk', Edinburgh TV Festival magazine, 1997.
7. Peter McGrath, 'The Facts Machines: Are We In Danger Of Information Glut'?, *Newsweek*, 6 June 1994, p. 33.
8. Saul Wurman quoted by Victor Keegan, 'Brain Storms'.

PLAY/WORK

1. Ned Polsky, *Hustlers, Beats and Others* (Harmondsworth: Penguin, 1971).
2. Johan Huizinga, *Homo Ludens* (London: Paladin, [1938] 1970).
3. Richard Neville, *Playpower* (London: Paladin, 1970).
4. Dennis Hayes, *Behind the Silicon Curtain: The Seductions of Work in a Lonely Era* (London: Free Association Books, 1989), p. 82.
5. Ibid., p. 136.

QUEER/ORDINARY

1. Susan Sontag, 'Notes on Camp' (1963), in *The Susan Sontag Reader* (Harmondsworth: Penguin, 1987).

RISK/SAFETY

1. John Schwartz, 'Blame Society, not the Net, for the Evils Lurking On-Line', *Washington Post* Business section, 18 November 1996.
2. Howard Rheingold, *Virtual Reality* (London: Secker & Warburg, 1991), previewed in *The Guardian*, 27 August 1991, p. 28.
3. Cotton Ward, 'Sitting Naked at the Keyboard', *.net*, September 1997, pp64–9.
4. Jim McClellan, 'Slash and Backlash', Wired (UK), October 1996, pp. 27–8.
5. Joia Shillingford, 'The Ugly Facts at Your Fingertips', Online supplement, *The Guardian*, 23 November 1996, p. 7.

SUBJECT/OBJECT

1. Robert Longo quoted in the press pack for *Johnny Mnemonic* issued by Twentieth Century Fox, London, 1995.
2. William Gibson, *Neuromancer* (London: Victor Gollancz, 1984).
3. Douglas Rushkoff, *Cyberia: Life in the Trenches of Hyperspace* (London: HarperCollins, 1994), p. 225.
4. Gwyneth Jones, 'The Neuroscience of Cyberspace: New Metaphors for the Self and its Boundaries', paper to the

Governance Of Cyberspace conference, University of Teesside, April 1995.

5. Ibid.
6. John Perry Barlow quoted in Mark Slouka, *War of the Worlds: The Assault on Reality* (London: Abacus, 1996), p. 13.
7. Ibid.
8. University of Arizona student quoted by J.C. Herz, *Surfing on the Internet: A Net Head's Adventures Online* (London: Abacus, 1994), p. 224.
9. John Perry Barlow quoted in Rushkoff, *Cyberia*, p. 11.
10. Sadie Plant, *Zeros+Ones: Women, Cyberspace and the New Sexual Revolution* (London: Fourth Estate, 1997), reviewed in *The Modern Review*, October 1997, p. 67.
11. Kevin Kelly interviewed by Cooper James, 'Anthills of the Interface', *The Independent*, section two, 10 July 1995, p. 14.
12. Ibid.
13. Kevin Kelly, 'New Rules for the New Economy', *Wired*, September 1997, pp. 140–3 and pp. 186–97.
14. R.U. Sirius quoted in Rushkoff, *Cyberia*, p. 294.
15. Jones, 'The Neuroscience of Cyberspace'.
16. Roger Burrows, 'Cyberpunk as Political Theory', paper to the Governance of Cyberpsace conference, University of Teesside, April 1995.
17. Doug Kellner, 'Mapping the Present from the Future: From Baudrillard to Cyberpunk', in *Media Culture* (London: Routledge, 1995), p. 299.
18. Mike Davis, *Beyond Blade Runner: Urban Control, The Ecology of Fear* (Westfield, NJ: Open Magazine pamphlets, 1992), p. 3.
19. Manuel De Landa, 'Non-Organic Life', in J. Crary and S. Kwinter (eds), *Zone Incorporations 6* (New York: Zone Books, 1992).
20. Manuel De Landa, 'Virtual Environments and the Rise of Synthetic Reason', in Mark Dery (ed.), *Flame Wars* (Durham: Duke University Press, 1993).
21. Burrows, *op. cit.*

TECHNICAL/CULTURAL

1. Julia Thrift, 'Nothing Upstairs: The Utterly Suburban Bungalow Once Meant Dangerously Louche Living', *The Guardian*, Space supplement, 14 November 1997, p. 17.
2. Raymond Williams, *The Long Revolution* (New York: Harper & Row, 1966), p. 41.

3. Andrew Calcutt, 'Uncertain Judgement: A Critique of the "Culture of Crime" ', in *Marxism, Mysticism and Modern Theory* Suke Wolton (ed.) (London: Macmillan, St Antony's series), p. 30.

UNIVERSAL/PARTICULAR

1. Quoted from *Scientific American*, June 1954, in M. Kadi, *Welcome To Cyberbia* (Minneapolis: Utne Reader, March–April 1995), p. 57.
2. M. Kadi, *Welcome to Cyberbia* (Minneapolis, Utne Reader, March–April 1995), pp. 57–9, excerpted from *h2so4*, Winter 1994/Spring 1995.
3. Ibid.
4. Melanie McGrath, *Hard, Soft and Wet: The Digital Generation Comes of Age* (London: HarperCollins, 1997). Quoted in Brendan O'Neill, 'More Than Virtual', *LM* magazine, June 1997.

VIRTUAL REALITY/'VIRTUAL REALITY'

1. Barrie Sherman and Phil Judkins, *Glimpses of Heaven, Visions of Hell: Virtual Reality and its Implications* (London: Hodder & Stoughton, 1993), p. 25.
2. Bob Swain, 'Virtually a Perfect World', *The Guardian*, 14 June 1990, p. 31.
3. Eric Bailey, 'Dawn of Another World', *Daily Telegraph*, 5 May 1992.
4. Michael Heim, *The Metaphysics of Virtual Reality* (New York: Oxford University Press, 1993), p. 80.
5. Ibid., pp. xii–xiii.
6. Dr William Bricken, *Virtual Reality: Directions of Growth*, proceedings of Virtual Reality '91 conference (London and Westport: Meckler Ltd, 1991), pp. 1–6.
7. Mark Slouka, *War of the Worlds: The Assault on Reality* (London: Abacus, 1996), p. 101.
8. Simon Worrall, 'Anyone for Virtual Tennis', *Sunday Times* magazine, 26 May 1991, pp. 20–6.
9. Nicholas Schoon, 'Three Dimensional Close Encounters', *The Independent*, 3 June 1991, p. 4.
10. Bruce Sterling, 'Cyberspace TM', *Interzone*, November 1990, p. 62.
11. Dr John Waldern quoted in Eric Bailey, 'Dawn of Another World'.

12. Florian Brody, *How Virtual is Reality?*, proceedings of Virtual Reality '91 conference (London and Westport: Meckler Ltd, 1991), pp. 18–21.
13. Sterling, 'Cyberspace TM', pp. 54–5, 62.
14. Ibid.
15. Scott Fisher quoted in Worrall, 'Anyone for Virtual Tennis'.
16. John Perry Barlow quoted in Sherman and Judkins, *Glimpses of Heaven, Visions of Hell*, p. 168.
17. Sheila Johnston, 'Flights of Fantasy', *The Independent*, 22 June 1991, p. 30.
18. Sherman and Judkins, *op. cit.*, pp. 165–6.
19. Daniel J. Boorstin, *The Image* (London: Weidenfeld & Nicolson, 1962).
20. Robert Jacobson, president of World-Design, Seattle, quoted in 'Virtual Reality: How a Computer Generated World Could Change the Real World', *Business Week*, 5 October 1992, p. 55.

WAR/PEACE

1. Lt Colonel Martin R. Stytz, 'An Overview of Current Virtual Reality Research and Development Projects by the United States Department of Defense', paper to Virtual Reality Expo '94 (London, February 1994) (Westport and London: Mecklermedia Ltd, 1994), pp. 152–9.
2. Extract from press pack in James Der Derian, *Cyber-Deterrence* (San Francisco: *Wired*), September 1994, pp. 116–22.
3. Alvin and Heidi Toffler, *War and Anti-War* (Boston: Little, Brown, 1993), p. 3.
4. Der Derian, *op. cit.*
5. Kevin Robins and Les Levidow, 'Video Games and Virtual War', *New Statesman and Society*, 24 November 1995, p. 28.
6. Jean Baudrillard, *The Gulf War Did Not Take Place*, trans. Paul Patton (Sydney: Power Publications, 1995).
7. Toffler and Toffler, *op. cit.*, p. 4.

X-RATED/INFANTILIZED

1. Louise McElvogue, 'Porn on the 4th of July', *The Guardian*, Online, supplement 4 July 1996, p. 4.
2. Ibid.
3. Ibid.

4. 'Marketing Pornography on the Information Superhighway', research undertaken at Carnegie Mellon University, Pittsburgh, Pennsylvania USA, first published in full in *the Georgetown Law Journal*, quoted in Philip Elmer-Dewitt, 'Cyberporn: On a Screen Near You', *Time* magazine, 3 July 1995, p. 36.

5. Mike O'Brien quoted by Steve Gold, 'UK Group Fighting Net Porn Gets Rolling', *NewsBytes* 25 July 1997, NewsBytes News Network, http://www.newsbytes.com.

6. David Kerr quoted by Steve Gold, ibid.

7. Clive Feather quoted in Wendy Grossman, 'How to Keep Net Porn in Check', *Daily Telegraph*, Connected supplement, 5 August 1997, p. 10.

8. Jonah Seiger quoted by Mike Godwin, 'Free Speech 1, Censorship O: Looking Beyond the CDA Victory', *Wired (UK)*, September 1997, p. 94.

9. John Browning speaking at the Internet Developers' Association censorship forum, 9 September 1996, The Chelsea Hotel, London SW1 (author's notes).

10. Peter Dawe speaking at the same event (author's notes).

11. Text of the 'industry proposal' (p. 2) released at a press conference hosted by the Department of Trade and Industry (DTI), Victoria Street, London, on 23 September 1996.

12. Science and Technology Minister Ian Taylor as quoted in the accompanying DTI press release of 23 September 1996.

13. 'Editorial', *Business Week*, 10 April 1995.

14. Geoffrey Wheelwright, 'Ways to Protect Children from 'Net Pornography', Information Technology supplement, *Financial Times*, 6 December 1995, p. 8.

15. Nigel Bannister, technology editor, 'Parents' Hotline Fights Internet Porn', *The Guardian*, 1 July 1996.

16. David Kerr quoted in Robert Uhlig, technology correspondent, 'Internet X-Rating will Bar Children', *Daily Telegraph*, 1 July 1997.

17. David Lyon (Queen's Universiy), 'Cyberspace Sociality and Virtual Selves', paper to the Governance of Cyberspace conference, University of Teesside, April 1995.

18. Simon Davies speaking at a seminar on Civil Liberties and the Internet, King's College, London, 12 July 1996 (author's notes).

19. Bill Clinton quoted by Declan McCullagh, 'At the Censorware Summit', *Netly News*, 16 July 1997 (online).

20. Ibid.

21. DTI, 'Industry proposal', p. 4.
22. John Browning, 'How We Could Tighten the Net', *Daily Telegraph*, 28 October 1996, p. 28.

YOUTH/AGE

1. Paul McCann, 'Ulrika Has It. William [Hague] and Nicola [Horlick] Do Not. Welcome to Middle Youth', *The Independent*, 11 November 1997.
2. John W. Aldridge, *In the Country of the Young* (New York: Harper's Magazine Press, 1969), pp. 13 and 27.
3. For an extensive account of this transition, see Andrew Calcutt, *Arrested Development: Pop Culture and the End of Adulthood* (London: Cassell, 1998).

ZERO SUM GAME/EVERYTHING TO PLAY FOR

1. Anthony Giddens, *Beyond Left and Right: The Future of Radical Politics* (Cambridge: Polity Press, 1994), p. 49.
2. Anthony Giddens, speech to the Risk Society Conference, Institute of Contemporary Arts, London, March 1995 (author's notes).

Index